ALASKA
979.83
MIC

MAY 13 2004

S0-BDP-111

Eight Stars of Gold

PROPERTY OF
KENAI COMMUNITY LIBRARY

KERN COMMUNITY LIBRARY

Eight Stars of Gold

Betsy Mickey

VANTAGE PRESS
New York

FIRST EDITION

All rights reserved, including the right of
reproduction in whole or in part in any form.

Copyright © 2003 by Betsy Mickey

Published by Vantage Press, Inc.
516 West 34th Street, New York, New York 10001

Manufactured in the United States of America
ISBN: 0-533-14532-5

Library of Congress Catalog Card No.: 2003090492

0 9 8 7 6 5 4 3 2 1

Eight stars of gold on a field of blue,
Alaska's flag, may it mean to you:
The blue of the sea,
The evening sky,
The mountains, lakes
And flowers nearby.

Alaska's flag
To Alaskans dear,
The simple flag
Of the last frontier.

Contents

Long before Alaska was a state, we went up there to live.

We flew up in an old World War II cargo plane. We left Seattle from a military air base. A small bus had let us off at the gate, and now we walked in and out among planes parked in front of several hangars. Locating the right plane was our own business.

Our flight had no number. The plane did not pull up to the terminal. As far as we were concerned, there was no terminal. Our luggage was not weighed or sent out to the plane on a cart. We carried our own, three big suitcases and a bag for diapers.

We knew which plane to board only because an airman, in a hurry, took time to point to a big plane with its door open and the ladder down, sitting far out on the airstrip. This was our Alaskan plane.

There were no tourist or first-class sections, no stewardesses with pillows or trays. Our pilot maintained a radio silence toward us also. He did not bid us welcome or give us the usual estimated time of arrival, or later, ever tell us how high we were flying. We knew we had a pilot because the plane took off and flew. That was good enough for us.

The plane had only a few seats, and they were by the wings. A wooden bench went around the bulkhead at the front of the plane, and a crate of old and wrinkled apples sat in the middle of the floor. Cargo for Alaska filled the rear of the plane, and our luggage was tossed on the floor in front of that. A young airman handed each of us a box lunch as we got on board. The box lunch had a cheese sandwich and two

1

limp carrot sticks, and we had apples from the crate at the front of the plane to snack on.

There were four of us. Two little children, Sue and Joe, and one baby, Pat. I was their mother.

Sue looked out the window. Joe went up front, sat on the bench with the airman, and they ate apples and talked. Pat broke out in chicken pox and held a tiny stuffed pink pig.

We left Seattle on a crisp, sunny day in early November when thoughts of Thanksgiving were just beginning to cross people's minds. But as our plane flew farther and farther north, the sky got darker and darker.

We flew through wispy clouds and fog. We could see ice form on the wings. When the clouds and fog cleared for a bit, we looked down to see nothing but thousands of acres of black trees, and rivers with ice along their banks. There were no lights from any city. No lights at all. Underneath the plane there was only freezing wind, clouds and fog, and far, far below, the wilderness. We were glad for the dim light in the cabin of the plane, the box lunches, the pink pig, and the box of apples on the floor.

We flew through two time zones and for six hours.

As we made our approach to Elmendorf Air Force Base to land, we flew over Anchorage. It had a few lights. At least we knew somebody was down there. Elmendorf had beacons and runway lights. Everything else was pitch dark.

The plane banked to land. We all had our coats and mittens on. I held Pat. But just as we neared the ground and could see the runway close beneath us, a fighter plane cut in ahead of us with his red lights flashing into our windows. He took our landing space. We had to go up, circle a few times, and try again. Our pilot probably swore under his breath, but he seemed to be the only one concerned. Nobody

2

else paid any attention. Except for Pat. Each time our plane came down, Pat, with her chicken pox, threw up.

But yet, we were here. The plane parked out on the airstrip. The ladder was lowered on the side away from the nearby hangars, so even the light from within the hangars did not reach us.

When we stepped off the bottom rung of the ladder, the snow-packed airstrip seemed to be the hardest ground on which we had ever stood. The plane towered above us, and looking up, we could still see the light in the cabin windows, the same windows from which we had looked down on icy rivers and the black trees. The dim light on the snow from the cabin was all that was left of what was familiar.

Outside our small circle of light, we were hedged in by a pitch-black night. I thought of small things. In their houses, had Alaskans eaten dinner yet? How would I ever get my coat clean? Perhaps it was after dinner after all.

Then Wes stepped out of the darkness. He hugged the kids and the kids hugged him. But he shook my hand and patted Pat on the head because of our soiled condition. This began our Alaskan living. We stood in the night with our breaths turning to frost and were glad to be together.

Our first winter, we lived in Nunaka Valley, just outside of Anchorage. Since the streets were covered with snow, we didn't find out until spring that they weren't paved. There were no street lights either. We could buy bread and milk and odds and ends at a house turned into a store in the valley. We bought mending thread there in a little tin box with a picture of Elizabeth on it. She had just been crowned Queen of England.

We had a little house, but we had no furniture. All we had were five borrowed cots from the army, a foot locker with a small black-and-white TV sitting on it, and a wringer washing machine that we rolled through the empty rooms out to the kitchen to do the laundry. Our own furniture was on a ship somewhere, coming slowly up the coast from the States to our house.

Even in our empty house, though, we learned a few things about Alaska. On our black-and white TV, we heard about people going outside for the winter. We couldn't understand what the fuss was all about. *We* went outside for the winter. We walked through the snow. We went to do our grocery shopping. Then we found that to go Outside meant to leave Alaska and go to the States. To Alaskans there was only Alaska—every place else was Outside.

We also got used to lots of dark. The sun rose after nine o'clock, so it was easy to oversleep. It was dark before three o'clock in the afternoon. Alaska was so far north that the sun was just above the horizon during the winter. Sunsets lasted for hours. We could see the Chugach Mountains from the windows of our house. The snow on the mountains was turned faintly pink by the setting sun. The evening star hung low over the mountains and sometimes a new moon also. And it stayed that way. We could watch TV or wash the clothes, but when we looked out the windows again, the pink mountains and the star and the pale rose-colored clouds were still there.

But what we wanted to see was Anchorage. We had always lived in cities. We had lived in Boston, New York, Chicago, Miami, Philadelphia, and Seattle. Anchorage was the biggest city in Alaska.

On our little TV, we had seen commercials from Monty's Department Store. "The biggest department store in Anchorage," the commercial said. We knew what to expect from "The biggest department store."

Department stores meant people pushing to get on elevators, glowing chandeliers hung from vaulted ceilings,

4

glitter and lights and the smell of perfume. Department stores had pink satin pillows where you rested your elbow while a salesgirl fitted you with a pigskin glove, and dim floors far above with only a single mannequin here and there and prices you wouldn't believe, and wooden soldiers in red coats that you could wind up and dolls of rare perfection by Madam Alexander.

One late afternoon under a night-time sky, we took a small bus from Nunaka Valley to Anchorage. The bus was nearly empty. We made no other stops. We just drove along in the dark. The bus was dim and quiet inside, and outside it was dark and quiet.

When the bus stopped, everybody got off. This was the terminal. The terminal was nearly empty too. There was a bus to take servicemen to Fort Richardson and Elmendorf. Now there was our little bus. There was no voice over a loud speaker calling out names of busses and giving departure points. A couple of wooden benches, floors that badly needed sweeping, a few sleeping natives, and some servicemen, all looking the worse for wear—this was the terminal.

Monty's Department Store was next to the bus terminal. The commercials had said so. There were snow drifts and darkness on one side. So we tried the other. The terminal building was divided in half, and the second half held a dingy room with a couple of racks of jeans and flannel shirts, rifles on the wall, and some pots and pans. The only salesperson in sight was a scowling little man who looked as though we had annoyed him by coming in.

We felt Monty's must be next door, that perhaps this was just part of the terminal. But next door was a bar, and then another bar, and a bar after that as far down the silent street as we could see. Even the bars didn't look friendly. The only lights were blue lights from electric beer signs over the doors.

5

We walked down the street. As long as we had come this far, we didn't want to miss anything. But there were no crowds of jostling people, no taxis, no clanging streetcars, no red and green traffic lights to brighten the dark. There were no rows of shop windows to look into. There was only packed and dirty snow with the flicker of a blue light now and then.

We walked back up the street past the store that was Monty's—the biggest department store in Anchorage—to the terminal next door. We had seen Anchorage and we were glad to get on our small bus and go back to our Nunaka Valley house.

In mid-winter, Grandma came up by ship and so did our furniture. Grandma was small and cheery and apt to wear pink dresses and soft little red walking shoes. We were glad to see her, and she was glad to see us, but she was still upset because the sticky buns they'd served on board ship had been so delicious and she'd gotten seasick after the first day out and hadn't been able to eat any more of them.

As soon as our furniture arrived, we took a big easy chair and our refrigerator to a trading post and swapped them for a car. Alaska was a great place for trading because pepole came and went a lot.

You don't get much of a car for an easy chair and refrigerator. Ours would start and it ran all right, but the heater didn't work and the defrosters cleared only a few inches of ice off the bottom of the windshield. Wes, who had expected better than this, drove hunched over the steering wheel, trying to see out of the little space that was clean in front of him. He kept saying, "This is exactly the way defrosters should work!"

The rest of us huddled under our blankets and peeked through our frozen windows and looked for moose. There were a lot of moose in Alaska—big bull moose with racks and cows without racks. Once we drove through Fort Richardson and past Elmendorf where we had first landed and drove on north to Eagle River. We saw a couple of signs by the side of the road that said "Caution: Moose." But we didn't see a moose that day.

We saw no people either. We saw no homes or buildings. We passed no other cars. We seemed to be alone in a frosted car in a strange and snowy world. At last we came to a small lodge at Eagle River. We turned around there and headed back to our house.

Spring/Summer

Once we got the car, though, we found that Anchorage did have a couple of places worth knowing about. Anchorage had a Piggly Wiggly. Now we could do a week's grocery shopping without running back and forth to the little Nunaka Valley store. But best of all, Anchorage had a Court House and in the Court House was the Land Office.

Alaska had just a handful of people, but millions upon millions of acres of land that didn't belong to anyone. In the Land Offices, we got papers that would allow us to claim two and half acres of land. Once our house was built on our land, we would return to the Land Office and be able to buy our land outright. The two and a half acres were called a Homesite.

The closest land open for Homesites was on Birchwood Road in a place called Chugiak. So far, we had seen Chugiak only on a map on the Land Office wall. It was farther north even than Eagle River.

You didn't need a road map in Alaska. One road went north. One road went south. We would go north to Chugiak.

Roads in Alaska had no billboards, or highway signs with speed limits or warnings of sharp curves or intersections (because there were no intersections). On the way north that day, we saw only one sign at the bottom of a steep hill with a sharp curve at the bottom. It said "Six killed here" and gave the date. Those road signs were the only ones Alaska had, but Alaskans figured they said everything that needed saying.

One early spring day when the sun was shining, we went to pick out our Homesite. The Chugach Mountains that we could see from the windows of the Nunaka Valley house went out to Chugiak and far beyond and back forever into the interior of Alaska. They were on the right side of the road. In the distance, on the left, was the Knik Arm that went in to Cook Inlet that went into the Pacific Ocean. The road to Chugiak went between the Chugach Mountains and the Arm.

We felt like old-timers when we got to Eagle River for the second time. When we passed Eagle River, though, we felt alone once more. The mountains did not get bigger or darker or move forward to overshadow the road, but they seemed to. We kept driving north. We felt we were in a strange and uninhabited land.

But today the sun was shining, and there was no ice on the windows.

We came to a lodge called Moosehorn. The Chugiak Post Office was in the lodge. The post office was a small shelf in a corner with pigeonholes at one side for the box holders. Alaskans paid federal taxes but couldn't vote in a presidential election. This cubbyhole of a post office was as close to the federal government as Alaskans in the boondocks came, or wanted to come.

Moosehorn was not fancy. It was a harsh and ugly place. There was no big fireplace and there were no easy chairs to pull up in front of it. The windows were large and curtainless and none too clean and looked on gas pumps and asphalt. The floors were of cement and had no rugs. There was a horseshoe-shaped counter facing onto an open kitchen. You could get coffee and sandwiches made by a short-order cook who filled in doing odd jobs when he wasn't needed in the kitchen. There were racks of anti-freeze, cans of oil, and a few loaves of bread for sale.

Off on one side, there were shelves of books, discarded by the Fort. This was the Public Library. One of the better things Chugiak had to offer, although we didn't know it at the time, was Marie MacDowell. The Public Library of discarded books was her doing.

We went farther north again.

Five miles down the road, we saw a school. We had expected to teach the kids at home. But this school had a flag waving out in front, a large snowplowed playground, and was made of red brick and was two stories tall.

We felt Chugiak had everything we would ever need.

Homesite land was on Birchwood Road, which went down a long, steep hill toward Knik Arm. A snowplow had cleared the road, but, like Nunaka Valley roads, under the snow this road wasn't paved either. We drove slowly down the road, opened the car windows, and leaned out. The wilderness was silent and smelled of wet woods and spring. There were birch trees and scrub pine and brush everywhere, still standing in deep snow. But there were deep hollows at the base of the trees because the snow was melting. Now and then, clumps of snow slid off the branches of the pines.

At the bottom of the hill, we got out of the car and walked on the road, looking at the land on either side. We wore low-topped shoes. We were going to build a cabin in this wilderness, but we didn't even own a pair of Alaskan boots and couldn't walk through the drifts left from winter. A red stake here and there, still almost hidden by snow, showed surveyor's marks for Homesite boundaries. We chose our two and a half acres from the road. We would walk on our land after the snow melted.

Our land was flat, and it had enough road frontage so that we would be able to get in and out next winter. The road would also bring a school bus for Sue for first grade.

Once more we felt we had everything we could possibly need.

At first, all the land had looked alike with birch and pine and brush. Once we chose our land, though, the land around didn't look the same anymore. Ours looked better than all the rest. In all the great territory of Alaska, we had two and a half acres.

We went back to our house in Nunaka Valley, but from then on, we had building on our minds.

We began to build our cabin on May 30, Decoration Day, 1955. Since the bulldozer that we hired for clearing the land was so small, we chose a little brush-filled clearing back from the road. The dozer could clear brush, but not much more. We would have trees all around the cabin. Also, to fit the cabin into the clearing, we would have to put it slantwise to the road, not facing it. We liked that too. One could drive down the road and not even know we were there.

Mr. Barnhardt delivered our first load of logs. He was a tall and very big man, and he had a sawmill far to the north, even of us. But the first thing he did after getting out of the cab of his truck was to open his heavy parka and show us the tiny dog he carried inside next to his flannel shirt. She was a Mexican Chihuahua. He told us her name was "Itty Bitty." He was so big and she was so tiny. Mr. Barnhardt was our first real Alaskan. We hadn't expected Itty Bitty at all.

Mr. Barnhardt put Itty Bitty back into the cab of his truck to make sure she stayed warm. Then he looked around him and saw he hadn't enough room to unload the logs. He said, "Let me get my ax." So he got an ax from the truck and with no fuss at all, he whacked down just enough trees to give himself unloading room. All this time we just stood there and watched. We couldn't think of anything to say.

We'd never met anyone before who carried an ax around with him. We were going to build a cabin, and we didn't even own an ax yet. And Itty Bitty watched us from the cab window. Mr. Barnhardt was one surprise after another.

We had never built a log cabin. We had never built a birdhouse or even put up a shelf. But we knew a house should be level and not slanted, so that was where we started. After Mr. Barnhardt unloaded his logs and left, Wes dug a little hole at each of the four corners of the cabin. Our cabin would measure twenty by thirty feet. We put a cement block in each hole and then another on top of that, extending above the ground a little. We ran a string from cement block to cement block and held a tool called a level on the string. We shifted the blocks around until the level told us the blocks were even. We were ready for the logs to go on.

The logs Mr. Barnhardt had brought us were called three-sided logs. Three sides of each log had been trimmed off at his mill. Our logs would stack together close that way. The one round side would be on the outside and make our cabin look like a cabin.

The first log we laid down all the way around was called "the sill." The second log was much wider. Floor joists would be set on the second log.

We carried each log, which was heavy, from the edge of the road where they had been unloaded back to our little clearing. Wes walked at the middle of the logs, taking most of the weight. The rest of us trailed along at the end of the logs, trying to hold them off the ground. But even then, soon there was a trail where the logs bumped along over roots and knocked down brush.

By the time we had leveled the blocks and laid the sill and the wide log, we felt we had done a lot. And we had.

After that, we drove from Nunaka Valley to Chugiak every evening and worked on the cabin. Wes worked all day for FAA (Federal Aviation Agency) at Fort Richardson, but after dinner we would go to our land and work till midnight. Even at that time of night, there was only a pale twilight. One could read a newspaper without turning on a lamp. Since we were working with logs and big spikes, we had no problem.

We got tired, but the rent on the Nunaka Valley house was due on July 15, so we didn't take time to think about how tired we were. We wanted to move into the cabin on the fifteenth, and we would have liked to have as much of a roof over our heads as possible.

Our neighbors in Nunaka Valley were newcomers, just as we were. They had trouble sleeping because it never got really dark. They would tack blankets over the windows to keep out the light, but nothing worked for them. They would ask us, "How can you sleep?" but we were so tired that we just closed our eyes and slept with no problem at all.

And every night we kept building under a sunset sky that never changed.

After we had laid the sill and the wide log, we laid another log on top of that. Floor joists would be nailed to the wide log and butt up against the log above it.

Before the walls got any higher, the floor had to be laid. Before the floor was laid, we had to put in the floor joists.

Joists are boards that are thick and sturdy and get nailed in place on their sides instead of lying flat like most other boards. We drove long nails slantwise through the joists to fasten them to the wide log. Nailing things this way is called "toe-nailing," but we don't know why. Joists are placed sixteen inches apart. They are not put close together.

After all the joists were secured, we could walk over them, stepping from one to another, just like stepping-stones, and still see the ground underneath.

We nailed the floorboards over the joists. Once we

started laying the floor, we seemed to be building a home. For the first time in this wilderness, we would be walking on clean white boards lying side by side, nailed in place and smelling of fresh cut lumber. On our floor we were not stumbling over roots and fighting brush that clung to our jeans.

Wes had heard that a good carpenter could drive a nail in using only three strokes. Nails for the joists had been so long that we had something to hold onto while we pounded. But flooring nails were a lot shorter and hard to hold steady enough to get a swing at. We found that flooring nails can fall over if you don't hit them hard enough to tap them in. We found that they can bend and have to be pulled out. They can also go in slantwise and then the nail will not go entirely into the wood. You can stub your toe on this one. Worst of all, we found that sometimes we hit hard with the hammer, missed the nail, and hit our fingers and thumbs. By the time the whole floor was laid, white and clean under the Alaskan sun, we could drive a nail with three blows of a hammer.

Right then, if we had to leave Nunaka Valley and move out to our land, we would have a floor to walk on and not get our feet muddy.

We started laying the walls. The fifteenth of July hung over our heads, but with each log we raised, the wall got higher. Each log was nailed in place with twelve-inch spikes pounded in by a ten-pound sledgehammer. The logs overlapped at the corners and formed a sort of ladder.

We had no architect and no house plans. We left room for doors and windows as we went along and wherever we thought it was a good idea. Spaces for the windows were left open close to the floor. We wanted our little kids to be able to walk right up to any window in the house and look right outside without ever having to stand on tiptoe. Alaska was too beautiful to be just kept out of doors.

The kids were so little that when we built, they stayed in the house in Nunaka Valley with Grandma, who loved them. Grandma must have had serious doubts about all of us coming to Alaska. She must have had even more serious doubts about building a log cabin in the boondocks. Grandma was as city as we were, and she had been like that for a lot longer. But she never said a word. She just stayed as cheery and perky as ever. Grandma was a good sport.

And Wes and I laid log upon log.

One day we got bored with putting logs down all the way around the cabin. The wall was about halfway up, and we wanted to see how one high wall would look. So we cut a long log into short pieces and stacked the pieces on one corner between where we figured two windows would go. Soon we had a wall up, looking kind of like a thin tower. We were tickled at how easy this was. We would go back to heavy log-laying. But not that day.

We were still bored after this, so we dug space for a small garden at the back of the house. Seeds were hard to come by, but we got a package of cucumber seeds and bought six tomato seeds for fifty cents from an open pack in the general store. In Matanuska Valley, north of us, vegetables, like cabbage, did grow. They grew larger than those in the States. But cucumbers and tomatoes were not among the vegetables that grew in Alaska. Especially any planted from seed at the end of June in a far northern place.

Later on that lazy, loafing day, Mr. Barnhardt came again with another load of logs. We showed him our little tower of a wall. We showed him the garden in back and told him about the tomato and the cucumber seeds.

About the wall, Mr. Barnhardt looked very serious. He told us that the logs weren't all the same thickness. By cutting just one log into short pieces and stacking it up, we might not come out even with all the other logs that went into place one by one. He also said that two windows so close together meant the corner wouldn't have enough support. So we would have to tear our foolishness down.

Mr. Barnhardt also walked around the cabin and looked at the other logs we had already put in place. We hadn't peeled the bark off the rounded part of the logs facing the outside of the cabin. Mr. Barnhardt looked very serious again. He told us the bark had to come off or the logs would rot. We didn't know this, and besides, we were in a hurry. Now we knew better. We would buy a wood chisel, and from then on we would peel the logs before we put them up. Peeling green logs was a pleasure. The bark came off in long glistening strips and smelled piney from the resin. But the bark on the logs already in place had dried. Long after we moved into the cabin, we would be peeling that inch by inch and leaving skin from our bruised knuckles behind.

When it came to the garden, Mr. Barnhardt didn't look serious at all. He looked downright twinkly. His eyes crinkled as though he were going to laugh. He pulled at his beard and looked away at the forest. He knew that neither tomatoes nor cucumbers would grow. But he had already told us the bad things we needed to know. He cleared his throat and said, "Cucumbers and tomatoes will be real nice. They'll come in handy for a salad. Good luck on your garden." Mr. Barnhardt had a kind heart.

The days went by and the days turned into weeks.

One day we sat on a half-raised cabin wall to eat our lunch from a sack. A cow moose and a calf trotted through our clearing and past our cabin as though we weren't there. The calf rolled his eyes at us but stayed right by his mother's

17

side. The cow held her head high, and she never looked to the right or to the left. She looked straight ahead toward the wilderness on the other side of the clearing. She didn't go any faster or any slower. She acted as though the whole place was hers and we were there for just a moment or two. Generations of her ancestors had made the trails around the cabin. The land belonged to her no matter what papers the Land Office had given us.

One day Wes had a holiday from work. We left Nunaka Valley early so as to get a lot done on the cabin. With the first whack of the sledge hammer, the handle broke off. We had to go into Anchorage to replace it. That was the way the day started. It never got any better. we had a flat tire. We ran out of spikes. Wes smashed a finger. We made three trips into Anchorage. We ended with nothing more done that day than when we started.

One day the Electric Company truck came to our cabin and two Electric Company men hooked up the cabin for electricity. The walls weren't all the way up. We didn't have any wires or outlets in the cabin. We didn't even have a roof. But when we did have them, we could have electricity.

The cabin walls got so high we used a rickety stepladder to get the logs in place. Then, finally, one day, the walls were finished.

We still had two more logs to raise. These would be the beams.

They would go across the center of the cabin and support the roof. These were the great beams. They were the grandfathers of all logs. They were round and not three-sided and when we peeled them, they were pale gold in color and glistened in the morning sun.

For once, we needed help. One beam was sixteen feet long and would go across the living room. The second beam

18

was ten feet long and would go across somebody's bedroom. We could not raise such heavy beams by ourselves.

Crawford came out to help us. Crawford had a strong back. He was young and blond and friendly. He was cheery as a cricket. Looking at those great logs lying on the floor, we felt a little more hopeful with Crawford there.

With a wood chisel, we flattened one end of the longest beam. We raised that end into place in a niche that we had cut in the top log of the cabin wall. It fitted exactly.

Sixteen feet into the cabin, we put up a thick post as high as the ceiling and braced it to stand the weight of the other end of the beam. With all of us working together, we raised the second end of the beam and rested it on the post. We had flattened this end also, so it didn't roll. It fitted between the outer wall and the post as though it had grown there.

We raised the second beam the same way. This ten-foot beam went from a niche at the top of the opposite wall to a braced post ten feet into the room.

We would have a living room sixteen feet long under one pale gold beam. We would have a bedroom for someone under the ten-foot beam. We had skipped four feet between the two beams. Later we would have a four-foot stairway that would someday go up to the second floor.

We rested after the beams were in place.

Another day, we toe-nailed joists from the top of the beams to the top of the outer walls. Just as we had put joists under the floorboards, now we would put them under the boards that would cover the roof.

If we could have walked upside down like flies on a ceiling, we could have hopped from roof joist to roof joist and seen the Alaskan sky beneath us instead of seeing the ground as we had when we hopped across the floor joists.

Right now, the doorways had no doors and the window

19

spaces had no windows, but to go inside, we had to step through a doorway. We walked across a wooden floor. We stood by our windows spaces and looked outside. If you didn't look up, you would have thought you were in a cabin that was almost done.

Nailing roof boards in place was pretty easy, except that we were afraid of heights. We propped a tall ladder against the cabin and climbed up. The ladder shook somewhat as we went from rung to rung. At the top, we crawled onto the joists. Once a few roof boards were nailed down, we could still look below us into the cabin beneath, but the nailed boards gave us kneeling room. Then we just kept adding boards. By now, we knew how to sink nails with three blows of a hammer.

The roof kept getting bigger and bigger, but we were happier pounding nails in the middle of the roof than on the edge. From where we knelt on the roof, the driveway where Mr. Barnhardt had delivered our first logs looked small and far away. When we needed more nails or boards, we crawled over to them on all fours instead of standing up and walking. When we stood up, the ground seemed to drop away altogether. Even when laying the boards on the roof was finished, we were still afraid to stand up and look around. We just crawled to the edge where the ladder was and got to the ground.

But we had to go back up. This time we carried rolls of tar paper and pails of tar up on our shoulders. We covered the roof with the tar paper and nailed it in place. We covered the tar paper with the tar.

Later, when we had time, we would pull up both the tar paper and the tar. We would put up a tall roof with a steep pitch that would let the heavy snows slide off. The roof we worked on now would be our second floor. But right now, the flat roof was the only roof we had.

Once the roof was covered over, the inside of the cabin seemed dim. The sun shone onto the floor through the spaces for the windows and doors. The cabin was sunny and cheery. But we were used to working under the open sky.

A lumberyard had opened up in Eagle River. We weren't their first customers, but we came close. And what we bought was pure class. Instead of rough boards and logs, we bought three sheets of plywood. We got the best plywood that they had. It was walnut and brown and polished. In the Alaskan boondocks, this was posh. We bought windows that rated up there with the plywood. Instead of a single pane of glass, each window had nine small panes. We felt high and mighty.

So far the cabin was one big room. We hadn't put up any walls because we didn't know how to build them. But we needed one wall that would go up along the right-hand side of the stairway-to-be and give us bedroom space on the other side. We put the studs in place.

Studs are like joists except that joists go back and forth from wall to wall and studs go up and down from floor to ceiling. We nailed the plywood to the studs. Then we had a wall. It wasn't so tough after all.

On the living-room floor, we made board frames for each window and fitted them into the window spaces. When we built, we hadn't measured anything. We always said, "That's about right," and let it go at that. Now we found that "about right" wasn't good enough. The windows didn't quite fit. Wes had to cut the logs back at the window spaces to give the windows enough room. He used cross-cut saws and hand saws. Mostly, he used a lot of muscle. But the windows finally fit.

The windows still looked tacky from the outside. Even when they were in place, they looked unfinished. We had Mr. Barnhardt bring us long slabs. Slabs were what Mr.

Barnhardt had left over after he ran logs through his mill and made three-sided logs. We peeled the slabs and cut them to form extra large frames. On the outside of the cabin, we nailed the frames around the windows. Now each window looked like a picture in frame.

The outside of the cabin was getting pretty good-looking, even with no doors and a flat roof.

Wes wired the cabin. The wires were thick and heavy, but we ran them close to the floor so they wouldn't show. Wiring was clean and easy. We had never done such a big job with so little trouble.

We scrounged a small electric stove and another refrigerator to take the place of the one we'd swapped for the car. We would have a refrigerator with cold milk and eggs in it, an electric stove to boil our potatoes on and fry our steaks and bake our pies in, and we would have lamplight during the winter months when we needed it—but we would have no water.

We built an outhouse in the backyard. This was our bathroom. We got two five-gallon canteens from the army. There was a spring three miles up the road. The spring and the canteens were our water supply. Even when the spring froze over in the winter, we could still get water by breaking the ice. We got a big round tub called a number two tub, and it was big enough to sit down in to take bath. This was our bathtub. A teakettle on the cooking stove and a big kettle on the oil heater, we would get later would give us hot water. Ten gallons of water per day for six people can go a long way, once you get the hang of it.

One last thing needed doing before we moved in. We had no place to put our groceries or dishes or pots and pans. Since everything was either flown into Alaska or came in by ship, wooden crates were easy to come by. At our Piggly Wiggly, we got orange crates. Everybody else in Alaska could be drinking orange juice, but we would use the crates for kitchen cabinets.

The refrigerator stood to the left of the kitchen door. The little stove stood next to the refrigerator under the kitchen window. We lined up the orange crates next to the kitchen stove. This was July fourteenth, and we were feeling giddy. We stacked the crates one on top of another. We stood some upright and put some on their sides. We took the ones that had been on their side and put them upright. We put the upright ones on their sides. We had time to kill. We sat on the floor and rearranged crates, like kids playing with building blocks. When we were finished, we had a nice little wall section of kitchen cabinets.

We went back to the Nunaka Valley house to sleep for the last time. It made no difference to us. It was just another day. But the cabin was done well enough. It would house us all.

July fifteenth was the day of days.

Joe turned five years old.

We moved, all of us, to the cabin for good that day.

We saved paying another month's rent.

We borrowed a pickup truck and loaded it with furniture and clothes. For the last time, Grandma and the kids had to stay behind in Nunaka Valley.

At the cabin, we unloaded the furniture and put everything in the right place exactly. Our big crocheted rug on the living-room floor. Easy chairs by the windows. Dining-room table and chairs in a corner by the kitchen. The window in the dining room looked out to a mountain. Four beds and a crib on the other side of the wall in one big bedroom.

Wes left to return the pickup and to bring out Grandma and the kids. I stayed behind in the cabin.

Sue and Joe were wild with excitement on moving day.

They wouldn't have cared if all the furniture had been piled in the middle of the room. Pat was excited, too, but didn't know why. Wes and I were just relieved. But Grandma was a special case. We wanted the cabin to look right for her.

Grandma used to say "First impressions! First impressions!" and wag her finger. She meant "First impressions are lasting," but she said it often enough that we didn't have to hear the tag end. She also used to say, "Talk is cheap but it takes money to buy whiskey," but that didn't concern us right now. We wanted to ease the brunt for this city woman who felt that being more than a short ride on a street-car from Marshall Fields was to be out of town.

So, in a cabin silent for perhaps the last time, without either the sounds of hammering or the noise of children, I worked at putting everything away. I hung coats on nails by the back door. I hung clothes neatly on a pole across the corner of the bedrooms. I made beds and plumped pillows and smoothed comforters. I set the table for Joe's store-bought birthday cupcakes, each one with a candle. Six cupcakes, six candles, so he had one to grow on. I got coffee ready to perk with water from the canteen. And I tacked up a blanket over the kitchen door so Grandma would have at least one door out of two. I tried for homey. I tried with Grandma's "first impressions" in mind.

It worked too. Grandma and the kids got out of the car on this last trip. The kids raced in circles, a few times around the inside of the cabin and then out one door and in the other. But Grandma just stood in the doorway for a few minutes and looked over her new home. She walked slowly through both rooms. She noticed the made beds and the hung-up coats. She noticed every little thing. She smiled the whole time. We had done a good job. We had made a home.

We made one last haul to the Piggly Wiggly for groceries to last us a while. This time Grandma and the kids stayed alone in the cabin to look out of all the new windows, walk on the new floors, and see what the backyard looked like.

When we got back with the car full of groceries, everything at the cabin was deathly quiet. No kids in sight. Not a sound.

Once inside the cabin, Grandma stuck her head out from behind the wall. Her eyes were round and even her white hair looked sparked with energy. She was standing, clutching Pat, plastered against the wall opposite the kitchen door with the blanket tacked over it. Joe and Sue were squashed in behind her. They looked out, one on either side, pleased and interested.

Grandma said in a whisper that sounded hoarse, "There's a black bear in the backyard. I saw him. I heard an animal moving around. I could hear him snuffling. He scratched at things. I peeked out from behind the blanket and there he was—a big, black bear in the backyard!"

Could this be true?
You bet. There were black bears all over Alaska.
They usually live higher up.
Not this one. He came down.
We hadn't any food around. He's just curious.
Maybe.
If a moose can walk through our land, why not a bear?
Would he keep on going like the moose?
Not likely.
Bears are supposed to be fat and lazy at this time of year.
    Does that mean he'd be friendly?
Not on your life!
What does an unfriendly black bear look like?
Standing tall on his hind legs and getting taller every
    minute. With teeth. Lots of teeth.

We thought these things because thinking was easier

25

than trying to figure out what to do if the bear decided to come into the kitchen.

Then, even as we thought, two big black paws came in under the blanket. We all watched the black paws. Then there was a snuffling sound and a big black head came in. But this head had friendly eyes and a tongue lolling out of one side of its mouth. With the blanket pushed to one side, we saw the creature also had a wagging tail. It was a dog. A big black dog.

The kids popped out from behind Grandma where she had planned on protecting them single-handed against the bear. They played with the dog in the backyard. That day was turning out better than their wildest dreams.

The rest of us just sagged against the wall. We stayed there for a while. Grandma started to laugh. She never did say "Whose crazy idea was this Alaskan business anyway?" She just leaned against the wall and laughed.

So much for first impressions.

The dog left as suddenly as he had come. We never saw or heard from him again.

We all helped Joe eat his cupcakes. Six people, six cupcakes, six candles. Five for the birthday and one to grow on. In the quiet light of the evening, we each sat in our own place at our own table in our own cabin. As we would do for many years to come.

That night we slept well with doorless doors, but the next day, Wes made us doors to be proud of. The doors were made of three heavy planks each. Thick cross bars were nailed across the top and across the bottom. These kept the planks tight together. We put insulation between the cross bars and then nailed three more planks on top of them. These were the doors, and they were almost four inches thick. We bought the heaviest hinges we could find to bear the weight of these heavy doors.

Once the doors were hung, we had to figure a way to keep them from swinging open. They were homemade so they didn't have door knobs or locks. We drilled a hole in a piece of two-by-four. We attached this to the door with a bolt so we could move it up and down. Up, the door would open. We built a wooden latch on the door frame. When we pulled the two-by-four down, it fitted into the wooden latch and held the door tight shut. When we barred the door, nothing could get in at us.

Now we woke each morning in our sunny, curtainless cabin that still smelled of pine and fresh-cut lumber. Even our furniture, which was not new, looked familiar but new. We had time to explore. we found cranberry bushes back of the house. We went down Birchwood Road to Knik Arm where we could look out over miles of the Pacific Ocean and see Mount McKinley in the far distance.

Red raspberries grew along the roadside farther north, toward Palmer in the Matanuska Valley. They grew inland too, but the ones by the roadside were easy to pick. We made jam from them. There were two kinds of cranber-ries—high bush and low bush. The ones that grew in our backyard were low bush, so we picked them. Alaskans used to call rabbits "low bush moose." They did like their little jokes. We made pies from the low bush cranberries. Blue-berries grew inland and were harder to come by, but they were big and sweet. We ate them out of hand.

The salmon ran in July. We didn't have the big king salmon. We had pink, or humpbacks. They came in from the Pacific to spawn into Cook Inlet, and then to the Knik Arm. A few ended up a short ways into Peter's Creek where it joined the Arm. We walked across the mud flats to watch the salmon.

27

Even at low tide, the flats were kind of soggy, but they were covered with wildflowers and the air smelled salty. Always, through the clean, clear air, we could see Mount McKinley off to the east and hundreds of miles away. Peter's Creek was shallow inland, and we looked down through the water to see the humpback moving so slowly we could have picked them up in our hands. But there was no use to this. The humpback in Peter's Creek had already spawned and were dying. Also, by this time, they were apt to have worms. But once they had been far out in the Pacific where we would never go. Now they floated in Peter's Creek.

Now that we were encased in our house, whatever building we were doing at the moment merged with our daily living. We built walls in a corner of the big bedroom for what would be the bathroom one day. Right now, that was as close as we got to a bathroom.

When Grandma was a little girl, she had lived in a country house without water. Grandma knew the ropes, and she taught us how to manage.

When we came back from trips to the mud flats at the Arm and were thirsty, we drank water from a canteen and used a dipper instead of turning on a faucet and filling a glass. We learned to take only a small dipperful of water and drink it all, rather than to fill a whole dipper and throw some water out the back door.

After meals, we scraped the plates with a rubber scraper. We washed them in a dishpan filled with water from the tea kettle, hot and soapy. We rinsed them in a second pan filled with hot, clear water. Then the dishes were dried and put away. The soapy water was thrown out the back door. The rinse water was saved and would be re-reheated to become the soapy water for the next meal's dishes.

When we bathed, we put hot water from the teakettle

and cold water from the canteen into the number two tub. We filled the tub less than half full. We washed as fast as possible to keep the water from cooling down. We started with the cleanest kid first. Then the next cleanest. And so on. When the bathing was done, we washed socks.

Grandma knew all the angles. After a while we got the system down fine. We didn't even think about faucets anymore.

The rainy season came early that year. Alaskans always said Alaska had four seasons—mud, snow, dust, and rain. There was nothing dusty about Alaska except for the Alcan, the highway that wound from Alaska through Canada down to the States. But the snow and mud were true descriptions and now the rains came. It rained for days. The cabin held snug with its flat roof.

Then one late afternoon, I walked barefoot across the living-room floor and stepped on a wet spot. I bent down to check on the spot, and a drop of water hit me on the back of the head. We had a small leak in the roof. I got a little pan, put it on the floor under the drip, and from then on, we had a plink sound every time a drop of water fell into the pan.

Later, in the kitchen getting dinner, I looked across toward the living room again. Several other drops of water were falling and all from different places in the ceiling. None of them was a stream of water, but the drops came fast and close together. We got more pots and emptied the first one we'd put down, which was getting pretty full. Now the sound of plinks was all through the house. Some were higher-pitched than others. Not all the drops landed at the same time.

The leaks in the roof weren't partial to the living room. The bedroom was getting leaked on, too. By now we were down to catching drops in bowls and saucers that weren't much help.

We had to go to Anchorage for shelter. Anchorage had a hotel, and we would spend the night at least. We couldn't fix the roof till the rains stopped.

The rain gave no hint of letting up either. We could hear the steady patter of rain on the roof and against the windows, along with our own private rain inside the cabin.

We trailed through the rain out to the car. Nobody said anything. There was nothing to say. We just looked out the car windows at the rain and drove down the road, south, to Anchorage.

We had hardly passed Moosehorn when we all started to talk at once. We all said, "Let's go home," and "We want to go home!" So we did.

We were a lot happier getting out of the car than we had been getting into it. The cabin looked sweet with the logs wet and pale and the rain running down the windows with their little panes. The air was still and smelled of pine.

We found five places in the cabin that didn't have leaks, and we moved our four beds and our crib under the dry spots. Two beds were in the kitchen, side by side. The other beds were crisscrossed here and there wherever they had room. But at least they were all dry.

We emptied the pots and pans and bowls again. Then we crawled into our own beds, pulled the covers over our heads, and slept.

The next day the sun was shining and we re-tarred the roof. After that, when it rained we used pots and pans to catch the drips. When it didn't rain, we worked on the roof with our buckets of tar.

One morning when we were up on the roof, we spotted a man moving about on the land across the road. The land sloped down to Peter's Creek and the leaves on the trees were too thick to see much, but we could get glimpses of a flannel shirt now and then. We heard the sound of an ax. Brush was being cleared away. Someone had taken the homesite directly across from us.

In the beginning, we had missed crowds and noise. Now we were the next thing to hostile toward this single stranger and the sound of his ax. Something in us felt that all the land with in sight and hearing range was ours. A neighbor was the last thing we wanted.

When we came down off the roof, a man was standing at the bottom of the ladder, waiting. We hadn't seen him come up the drive. He hadn't called up to us. He was just standing there, waiting. In all the years we were to know Bill, we suppose we said, "Here comes Bill" and opened the door for him. But yet, it seems as if suddenly he would be sitting, quiet and peaceful in a living-room chair, as though he had just materialized. He was as much a part of the cabin as we were.

Bill was tall and slim and blond. Grandma always said he looked as though he should be in an Arrow Shirt ad, he was that handsome. He was about our age, but he had probably looked about that age on the day he was born and would look only that old when he died.

Standing there at the bottom of the ladder, he didn't apologize for moving across the road, but he didn't crow about it either as we might have done. Forests and space were important, he said. Alaska had more space than Wyoming, where he was from.

Bill never did say much, and what he said was in the quietest of voices. You had to listen or you would have missed something. His voice was a lot like the rest of him. Unless you noticed his being there, he might not have been there at all. Bill was sort of like the Chicken and the Egg.

Was he there first and then you noticed him? Or did you notice him first and then he was there?

This stranger was not bad at all.

Sometime later, a small trailer was moved onto Bill's land, onto the slope down toward Peter's Creek where we couldn't see it, even when we worked on the roof. Like everything else about Bill, we were never sure when the trailer went onto the land. Besides that, we had problems of our own.

Although it was only July, the gentle days of summer were over for us. We had work to do before winter. We had to get up a steep-pitched roof and a chimney. And the chimney had to go up before the steep-pitched roof.

We bought an oil stove and a stovepipe and a chimney, called a Van Packer. The Van Packer came in sections, so you could install it yourself. No one told you how heavy the sections were.

We put the oil stove in the living room next to the beam. Above the stove, we cut a hole in the flat roof to fit the first section of our chimney. We bolted heavy metal braces on the joists and lowered the first section of the chimney down through the roof until it rested securely on the metal braces. The stovepipe went from the oil stove to the start of the chimney. The great beam gave the ceiling strength.

Now Wes carried every other section of the Van Packer up to the roof and set them one on top of the next until the ceiling was the right height.

As he went up the ladder, rung by rung, slowly under the dreadful weight of each chimney section, Grandma always clasped her hands and said, "How strong Wes is! Wes is so strong!" We had never paid much attention before, but now we stopped and noticed. Wes was bowed under the weight of the chimney, and the ladder shook under the weight of them both. Wes was strong all right. We lined up next to Grandma and said, "Wes! How strong you are!" Wes never said anything. He was too busy to notice, we thought. But years later, he still told how strong Grandma always thought he was.

Now we had a brand-new oil stove to keep us warm through the winter. We had a stove pipe too. And a chimney that was awesome.

The rafters for our steep-pitched roof hadn't gotten to our house yet from Mr. Barnhardt's mill. We had an afternoon off.

The raspberries were at their peak. I went berry-picking with Mary Ann. Mary Ann was a newcomer, as we were. Marie McDowell had told Mary Ann of a great spot to get raspberries up on the mountain right behind Moosehorn. Mary Ann was afraid to go alone. We went together.

Wes was at work. I had left Grandma and the kids home because Marie had said the picking was rough. We were just two young women, using berry-picking as a way to loaf on a summer afternoon.

From Moosehorn's parking lot, we followed an old abandoned wagon road up the mountain. The mountainside had rock outcroppings. Devil's Club, huge plants covered with savage thorns, grew everywhere. Footing was uneven. Losing one's balance was easy to do.

But still, the day was warm and sunny. Mary Ann was pleasant company.

Someone, sometime, had evidently tried to clear a field. We picked our way down a ravine about six feet wide and up the other side, heading toward a windrow that was all that was left of the farmer's boundary at the edge of his field. The windrow was made up of felled trees, lying every which way, and stumps, and the whole thing was covered with overgrown raspberry bushes. Raspberries hung thick and red and big.

We picked along the windrow. We picked raspberries by the handful. We chatted in the sun while we picked. The air smelled warm and sweet. Our berry boxes were nearly full.

Suddenly, from under the felled trees and brush and stumps of the windrow, right at our feet, right at the tips of our sneakers, there was a growl. Not a growl like a dog can make. But a roar like the lion at the zoo makes while he waits for his feeder to throw him meat.

A big black bear, fat and full of red raspberries, had crawled into the windrow to take a nap. We had woken him. We had awakened him at close range. We were within inches of standing on his nose.

We didn't waste breath or time on screaming. We turned and ran. As she turned, Mary Ann, with great good sense, tossed her baskets in the air. But as I ran through the raspberries falling like a summer shower, on the heels of Mary Ann, all I could think of was *What a waste!* Facing possible death, or at least probable mutilation, I was not about to throw away my baskets full of berries.

As we reached the ravine, we had crossed so carefully on the way to the windrow, Mary Ann, who was a tall girl with long legs, sailed over the expanse and came down with about four feet to spare on the other side.

I was short and had short legs. When I saw Mary Ann's leap, I felt I was doomed. Never could I jump like that. I thought of looking behind me to see where the bear was, but turning my head took time I didn't have. So, pop-eyed and panting, with berry boxes held straight out in front of me, I reached the edge of the ravine and jumped. I didn't land with the room to spare that Mary Ann had, but I soared into space and came down on the other side.

We raced, side by side, back down the old wagon road, back to Moosehorn's parking lot. Two truckers were leaning against their trucks, talking to each other. All we could gasp out was "A Buh . . . A Buh . . ." Mary Ann helped out by pointing in a wild manner back up the mountain.

One trucker looked at the other and said, "Must have been a bear all right." Then they chuckled, got in their trucks, and left. We didn't care. We were standing on asphalt again. We were back at Moosehorn. Up on the mountain, the bear was probably back asleep.

We have always liked Satchel Paige. He said, "Never look behind. Something may be gaining on you."

That man knew what he was talking about.

The scare we had didn't last long. We were just glad to be safe at home. Even putting up the rafters seemed better than the bear on the mountain.

Mr. Barnhardt brought us forty-four rafters and a ridgepole. Each rafter was sixteen feet long. The ridgepole was thin and thirty feet long. The ridgepole would run the length of the cabin, and the rafters would be attached to it on either side. When all the rafters were in place, the ridgepole would be thirteen feet high. We would have a steep-pitched roof all right.

While the rafters were still on the ground, we notched the end of each one. The rafters had to be notched so the roof would extend over the edge of the cabin. When the last rafter was notched, it was time to do the building. We could not postpone putting up the steep-pitched roof any longer.

We were used to pounding nails, raising logs, patching leaky roofs, and lifting weights. We would never get used to heights. We tried to close our minds, knowing that it was up to us to do the building. But each night we wished that when we got up the next morning, the rafters, like a migratory flock of primeval birds, would have flown onto our roof and settled in place by themselves.

We would start putting up the rafters and the ridgepole on one end of the flat-topped roof and work our way across to the other end. Putting up the first two rafters left a lot to be desired. We nailed the notched ends to the outer edges of the roof. That was the easy part. The other ends had to be nailed to the ridgepole that would run thirteen feet high down the center of the roof.

We carried the stepladder up to the flat-topped roof and placed it at the absolute edge of one end. The stepladder had been old and rickety when we got it. Our using it for months hadn't steadied it at all. The ladder was six feet tall, shaky, and swayed back and forth.

I began to climb the ladder, rung by rung, not daring to think how close I was to the edge of the roof. Even at the next to top step, I still had one rung to brace my legs against. But I had to go higher than that. With the ladder moving beneath me, I stood on the very top step. Then I stood full height and tried to support the ends of the two rafters against the ridgepole as far overhead as my arms would reach. Wes stood one rung below me to nail the rafters to the pole.

Now the ladder was holding two people, two rafters, and a ridgepole. It shook like the leaves of an aspen.

Wes, who was strong-willed, told himself that he was standing on solid ground. My instincts were to reach down, grab the top step I was standing on, and never let go. The obvious possibilities of falling off the roof and breaking all our bones never crossed our minds. The simple fear of height crowded out all sensible fears.

The rafters were heavy and did not want to stay tight against the ridgepole to be nailed in place. We tried and tried. Wes was yelling, "Hold the goddamn things steady!" The sky seemed to circle and dip, and our world was rough-cut lumber and a ladder that swayed.

Then it was done. The ridgepole was nailed between the first two rafters. We clung to the ladder getting down. We sat on the roof and breathed heavily for a while.

Now that the ridgepole was supported, nailing the rest of the rafters in place down the length of the roof would be a lot easier. The work would only be hard and slow. We could handle that.

Once we got away from the edge, the rafters we nailed in place seemed like a cage around us and were comforting. We had something to lean against and grab if need be.

While we were up on the roof with the rafters, Slim Land was sitting inside the cabin. Slim was tall and gaunt and was a tad wild through the eyes. He had a kind of wolfish look. He and Bill had been friends and cronies for years. Slim was building the stairs that would go to the second floor when it was finished.

Slim was the best carpenter around. People said he drank too much, but Slim said he'd been injured in World War II and needed something to kill the pain. We didn't know which was right. All we knew was that Slim turned down our offers of coffee. He had a pint of whiskey beside him in amongst the boards and nails. He took a swallow of that now and then while he worked.

We wanted wide stairs, even in our small cabin, so we wouldn't have to go up and down Indian file. And that was just the way Slim built them. Even with the whiskey, the corners were all sharp and the stairs were all the same height. He did a fine job and the finished stairs were beautiful.

Now, when we came in the front door, we faced our wide staircase going up along our walnut wall. Left of the staircase was the great beam. Left of the beam was our new oil stove with a big teakettle sitting on it.

We looked classier than we had any right to look.

But the days were getting shorter now—closer to what

we were used to in the States. Just as we had the rent on our minds before, now thoughts of winter drifted through our heads even toward the end of July.

But if we were fighting rafters and ridgepoles and the thought of winter, Bill was not. He was standing out in the Arm, wearing hip boots and gaffing salmon. After Slim finished our stairs, he drove down to the Arm and watched Bill for a while without Bill noticing him.

Using a gaff was forbidden. You could use nets, but a gaff was illegal. For all that Alaska had mighty populations of salmon and moose and just a scattering of people, Alaska was fierce in its protection of wild game. Alaskan game laws were sudden death. Game wardens gave no warning. Even at a first offense, you got nailed with a $500 fine, lost your license, and watched your guns or fishing equipment get sold at public auction.

Slim just stood there and watched Bill for a long time. Then he moved within shouting distance and hid behind a tree.

Suddenly he leaned out and yelled, "Hey! You there!"

Bill's instincts were right on the nose. He fired the gaff as far out into the Arm as he could. He could make up some story about walking around in hip boots when he'd had time to think of one. But they couldn't hang him for the hip boots anyway. Once the gaff was gone, so was the evidence. Slim just leaned against the tree and laughed his head off.

Bill told us all this later. He chuckled as he told it. But he still regretted the loss of the fine gaff that was lying on the bottom of Knik Arm somewhere.

In August, the sockeyes came. Sockeyes were hordes of tiny black flies. They didn't come into the cabin. They waited up on the roof in amongst the rafters and the nails. They swam through the cranberry bushes and the forests.

During hunting season, within seconds after a moose was brought down, sockeyes filled the air over his carcass and made life miserable for the hunters.

Pounding in the last of the rafters, we wore flannel shirts with the cuffs buttoned and the collars pulled up. We wore hats with the brims pulled down. We wore bandanas over our faces, but even by your first coffee break, our eyes were red and swollen. The flies would be with us till frost.

The boondocks were full of mosquitoes too. Travel brochures don't tell you about them.

Once the rafters were up, Mr. Barnhardt brought us rough-cut one by sixes. These would go over the rafters just as the floor boards had gone over the joists.

The afternoon was warm and still and smelled of cranberry bushes and birch leaves that were starting to turn to gold. We unloaded the lumber, but we all felt lazy. We sat drowsy in the backyard because nobody, not even Mr. Barnhardt, wanted to get back to work. We talked of building and lumber, and then we talked of rumors.

Rumor had it that bands of servicemen had been joy-riding around at night, hassling the homesteaders in their remote cabins. Wes worked at night. I was alone with Grandma and the kids. I thought the rumors were pretty silly, but sometimes late at night if a car went slowly down Birchwood Road, I wondered. Mr. Barnhardt had heard the rumor too.

He asked if we had a gun. We told him the only gun we had was our moose-hunting rifle—a 30:06. I had fired it once, but the kick had nearly knocked me down. Mr. Barnhardt said I didn't have to fire it or even load it for that matter. Just jiggle it around a lot.

He made me practice saying, "Stop or I'll shoot," in a high and quivery voice. I had to pretend I was jiggling an imaginary rifle. Finally Mr. Barnhardt was pleased. he just grinned and said, "There isn't a man in the Territory who would stand up to a nervous woman waving a 30:06."

As usual, Mr. Barnhardt had all the answers. We don't know if it would have worked because we never had to try it. But we laughed a lot that afternoon, and that took care of the rumor as well as anything.

We nailed Mr. Barnhardt's one by sixes on top of the rafters just as we had nailed floor boards on the top of the floor joists. We were good carpenters now. At least we could pound nails into boards. Pounding the nails took time, but we were proud as we pounded. We were building a second story with space for two more bedrooms.

Once the boards were nailed over all the rafters, we went back to the Eagle River Lumber Yard where we had gotten our walnut wall and our nine-paned windows.

We couldn't afford shingles, and besides that, we didn't know how to shingle a roof. So we brought ninety-pound roofing instead. We didn't know why they called it ninety-pound, but they said it was the toughest grade they had. The tar paper we had first had been fifteen-pound. We had a choice of two colors. Red or green. We thought about getting red but switched to green to match the pine trees.

The ninety-pound roofing came in big rolls like the tar paper but was much heavier. The edges didn't rip at all. We unrolled the ninety-pound, put it over the ridgepole, and down the other side. We used roofing nails to pound it in place. We overlapped the next sheet a little and so on, down the length of the roof. The ends of the second floor still weren't closed in, and the stairway that Slim had built still went nowhere, like the rich man's stairway that the "Fiddler on the Roof" sang about. But we had a steep-pitched roof, green and dry, instead of a flat-topped roof that was neither fish nor fowl—neither proper roof nor proper floor—and covered with black tar paper that leaked.

The day after the roof was finished, we celebrated. *Gone with the Wind* was playing in Anchorage, probably for the first time. We had seen the first showing in Chicago decades before. Clark Gable said "damn" at the very end, and we had waited through the whole Civil War just for that astounding word. We had not been to a movie for a year. We would enjoy the film. The kids would enjoy the popcorn. We would all celebrate together.

But at the first hint of battle, the kids began to snuffle. First we were just embarrassed. We kept saying "It's only make-believe." But the crying reached full voice. Other people had paid good money, too, to see this epic show. We left at the beginning of the big scene with all the wounded soldiers lying in a great area in front of the railroad station. We hauled the kids down the aisles with them still trying to peer over their shoulders to see just how bad things were going to get.

These were the same kids who took plane flights, bears in the backyard, and drafty outhouses with rare good humor. But we had inflicted the Civil War on them. We were so ashamed that we bought more popcorn on the way out. The kids wept all the way to the car, but once the car doors were closed and we pulled away from the curb, the weeping stopped and all we could hear was the sound of the chewing of popcorn.

We would have felt guilty all the way home. But a wind had started to blow. We hadn't heard it in the theater, but the farther north we got, the stronger it blew. Trees were down. Shingles were off at Eagle River.

If the kids had been scared in the movie, we were scared now. Gusts raged more than sixty-five miles an hour and shook the car. All we could think of was the roof, our brand-new roof. All the months of work. The money too. There was no one who would tell us this was only make-believe. Driving down Birchwood Road, things got even scarier. The wind was funneling down from the mountain we could see from our dining-room window. It funneled down the power line leading to our house. The roof would get full force.

When we pulled into the drive, the roof was still standing, steep and new and green. The cabin was still under it. The wind had hit the roof with full force, but the ends of the second story were still open and the wind blew through one end and out of the other. The roof had stood firm. Which was more than we could do at the time. Our legs were shaking.

One stormy, blustery afternoon in late August, I was in the kitchen baking a cranberry pie from berries we had picked out in back of the cabin that morning. The berries were coming to an end, but there were still enough for a pie or two.

The sky was gray. The clouds were low. The pie was bubbling in the oven. The smell of the baking pie was all through the cabin. Grandma left the bedroom where she'd been reading. The kids got up off the living-room floor where they'd been playing with games. They all moved closer to the kitchen. We handed out plates and forks. We took the pie out of the oven and set it steaming on top of the stove.

Suddenly, there was a figure at the window above the stove. A figure with outstretched wings, wild eyes, and a vicious, curving beak. There was a crash and glass cracked and splintered all over the top of the stove and the cranberry pie. The figure hurtled into the kitchen and landed in a heap on the floor.

It was a big hawk. The hawk must have seen some movement or reflection inside the window that caused it to dive. It lay on the kitchen floor and didn't move. We watched and watched, but it didn't move a muscle. The hawk's neck had been broken and it was dead.

We were sorry it was dead, but then a live and angry hawk in our small cabin could have been a problem. We put his body on a board and carried him outside under the trees where he had lived.

We swept up the glass. We covered the broken windowpane with cardboard for the time being. We threw out that delicious pie. We baked another one. That second pie was just as delicious as the first one would have been.

Fall/Winter

When Crawford, who was a soldier at Fort Richardson, neared the end of his tour of duty, he wanted to go panning for gold. We owed him one for helping with the beams. Besides, taking a holiday suited us fine. We would leave Pat with Grandma, who decided that, after all, gold-panning was not really for her or for Pat either.

We made sandwiches, a chocolate cake, and a big bowl of potato salad. We took thermos bottles of coffee and milk. We took pie tins for panning for gold.

We were going far north, but this time we didn't mind a bit. Now that we lived in the boondocks, we felt like real Alaskans ourselves.

Moosehorn habitues had told us about an old abandoned gold mine, north of Palmer, north even of Talkeetna. We would leave the highway that kept going north and follow the old mining road instead. The day was half light drizzle, and the clouds were overhanging. We didn't care. We would spend the day eating chocolate cake and panning for gold.

We took the 30:06, too. It wasn't hunting season, but we were going into grizzly bear country and the ways of grizzlies were not to be tampered with. We did not go hoping to see a grizzly, even at a far distance. The Latin words for grizzly are *Ursus horribilis*. And that was the way we felt about meeting one.

Grizzly bears can be nine feet tall and weigh over a thousand pounds. Grizzlies are also speedy and can go up to thirty miles an hour. They are bad tempered and crafty. Each year, grizzlies accounted for the loss of hunters who, when stalking them, found to their horror that the grizzly had stalked them also.

We never knew a real Alaskan who went after grizzly. Grizzlies weren't good to eat. They loved salmon and were apt to taste fishy. At least, that's what we were told. Alaskans hunted for meat on the table, and there was ample meat available without going through the shenanigans of going after a grizzly bear.

Alaskans left that for the trophy hunters who spent sums on bush pilots and guides. We were polite to trophy hunters because of the money they had to spend, but every time a grizzly got a hunter and we heard about it on the evening news, Alaskans would grin quietly to themselves. It was one up for our side. Grizzlies didn't waste money on big guns and bush pilots. Best of all, grizzlies didn't brag about getting a hunter.

We were in high spirits as we drove north. We had a lot to eat and the remote possibility of finding nuggets of gold. Finally we drove past a hotel/roadhouse/general store/gas station combination and then turned off onto the old mining road. When the mine had been in operation, the lodge would have been a going concern. Today, it was almost abandoned.

We followed a small creek for miles. We would pan in the creek. We looked for a place to stop the car and set up our picnic lunch. Suddenly as we drove north a front wheel caught in a soft spot and the car rolled over, tumbling down toward the stream. Instead of looking out the windows, as we had been, we were upside down, looking at potato salad on the roof of the car.

We counted noses and came up missing Joe. In my stunned condition, I poked with a finger into the mound of potato salad as though to uncover him somewhere under crumpled boiled egg and bits of parsley. There was a knock at the window and there was Joe. He had crawled out of the half-opened window and scooted up the embankment. We lowered the window the rest of the way, and we all crawled out and up the bank to the road. We got the 30:06 out, too.

We were ringed by mountains, but there the land was sloping and treeless. We looked out over the brownish gray sedges and hummocks of the tundra. We began walking back down the old mining road in the direction of the lodge. We held the kids' hands. Five of us, spattered and bedraggled by potato salad and chocolate frosting and the drizzle that was turning more to rain. Crawford carried the 30:06 against his shoulder. All we needed was a fife and drum.

A tow truck from the lodge fished the car out from between the embankment and the stream. The rear window was out. We cleaned off the roof as well as we could. We never did get that rear window fixed. We stuck in a piece of plastic and drove the car like that from then on. We had a bowl of soup at the lodge and got dried off a little while we watched the drizzle-rain come down outside. Then we drove home.

When we first found out that we were going to Alaska, we were standing in our kitchen in Seattle. Wes came home and told us. For a second, the kitchen disappeared and I had a quick glimpse of huskies pulling a sled through driving snow. My subconscious mind had probably latched onto Balto and his mighty effort to save Nome. The huskies and the blizzard vanished and I was back in our warm kitchen in Seattle. The sun was coming in the windows. Alaska was a name in a geography book—not even a name on any road map we'd ever seen. But the name "Alaska" had a nice ring to it. Besides, we'd never been there.

If we had known then what we knew now, we might

have had second thoughts. Alaska had close to 600,000 square miles of territory and was about the size of one-fifth of the whole United States. But moving around on all those square miles were fewer than 200,000 people. Fewer people than lived in Seattle. We had always thought of Seattle as a nice little town. Move the whole town to Alaska and you would have doubled the Alaskan population. If we had known this, we might have felt that we'd be rattling around like peas in a kettle drum.

Less than a year ago, we had flown over thousands of acres of wilderness darkened by a wintry sky, but half our minds had been occupied with cheese sandwiches and pink pigs. We had not stood on the ground and looked up at snow-covered trees or the icy mountains that rose beyond them. We had not known of tangled and ancestral trails that crisscrossed the forests, or the moose and bear that walked on them.

Chugiak was, after all, only twenty miles north of Anchorage. But we had tiptoed that distance, first to Eagle River and then to Chugiak. When we built, we had been occupied with thoughts of our hammer and saw and the piney smell of logs lying on the ground, waiting to be put in place.

But walking those slow and isolated miles back to a nearly abandoned lodge, we had thought seriously of grizzly bear for the first time in our lives. We had looked out over miles of brown and autumn tundra to a rim of mountains in the distance—mountains with glaciers filling the valleys between them, glaciers whose edges melted in late summer and filled the rivers and froze again in winter, traveling from age to age down to the ocean. We had looked off to mountains made of rock, with little vegetation—mountains with crevices and chasms and pinnacles and crags, where the Dall Sheep and the Big Horn were.

We had gotten no gold that day. But, in a sense, we had come face to face with Alaska.

In September, Sue started first grade. She had had a few weeks of kindergarten in Seattle. The night before we took the plane to Alaska, the school had a parent-teacher's meeting and, for some reason, I went, even though my child would never be in their school again.

I had walked up the steep Seattle hill in the November dark to where the school was with all its lights on. I was early, so there were only voices at the end of the hall, but the halls were empty and so was Susie's room. I stood alone and saw the little desk where Sue had sat. I looked at some drawings she had made in crayon.

While she was in kindergarten, she had learned a little song.

Let's go walking,
    walking, walking.
Let's go walking,
    far, far away.
Let's go back the way we came,
    the way we came,
    the way we came.
Let's go back the way we came
    Before.

We would be walking far, far away, but we wouldn't come back the way we came.

I had gone back down the hill in the dark to the Seattle house.

Now Sue started school again in Alaska. We had planned on taking Sue's hand and walking her out to the end of the driveway. We would tell her the bus knew where it was going and that someone would help her find her first-grade class room.

But Sue was having none of it. She didn't even want us to wave. She stood alone, straight as a ramrod, watching the bus as it came down the road. The four of us who were left behind peeked out from the sides of the windows in the cabin.

The yellow bus lumbered up to the drive, opened its jaws, and swallowed Sue. When school was over, the yellow bus spit Sue out again.

After the first day, it was all routine.

One day, doing our shopping at Piggly Wiggly, we changed our lives. We picked up a free pamphlet from the Fleishman Yeast people. The pamphlet told how to bake bread at home. We knew that great-grandmothers could bake bread. But we didn't know that anyone else could.

Yeast was kept in the refrigerated section at Piggly Wiggly. Little cakes of yeast, each about an inch square, wrapped in colored paper with the name "Fleishman's" written on top.

Next morning, we put all the ingredients the recipe had called for on the dining-room table. We needed the working room. Then we began to make bread dough.

As usual, Grandma was a help. When she was a little girl in the country, she had watched bread-making many a time. She had never made any bread on her own, but she remembered what she had seen. When I mixed the yeast with lukewarm water, Grandma said, "Don't have the water too warm! You'll kill the yeast!" The small cube I held in my hands was alive? "Of course," said Grandma. "What did you expect?"

We melted shortening in hot milk, added a little sugar, and let that cool to lukewarm, too. We mixed the milk mixture with the yeast and water. We added cups and cups of flour. After a while, the dough didn't stick to the sides of our big Ironstone bowl anymore. We had made bread dough.

So far, it had been simple. Now we had to learn how to knead. The pamphlet had pictures of kneading, with directions under each picture. We looked at the pictures. As we began to knead, Grandma read the directions step by step.

Kneading had a knack to it. We put flour on an old bread board we'd gotten from Great-grandma. We floured our hands too. We put the dough in the middle of the board, patted it into a flat circle, folded the circle in half, pressed it down with the heels of our palms, turned it a quarter of the way around, folded again, pressed, turned. Pretty soon we had a rhythm going. Fold, press, turn.

Soon the dough had a satiny look to it, like the directions said. We put the kneaded dough back into the big mixing bowl, spread a clean dish towel over the top, and put the bowl in the sun from the window over the kitchen stove.

I turned the page in the recipe booklet, expecting to find something really difficult to come next. But our part was over. Now the yeast that was alive took over. We had never done anything so easy in our lives.

In an hour, we didn't recognize the bowl as the same one we had put in the warm place. The dish towel, instead of lying flat, had a bulge. Under the towel, the whole bowl was filled with dough, round and smooth and up over the brim of the bowl.

I thought in a wild way, of the bedtime story of the little pot that wouldn't quit making porridge, even when the porridge flowed out of the kitchen and through the streets of the town. But the recipe said "punch down," which we did and the dough flattened out immediately. I was relieved.

The recipe said "Let rest for ten minutes." Even then we were to be considerate of the yeast that had been working silently and mightily for the past hour. After the dough had rested, we shaped two loaves, put them in tins, covered them with towels, and put them back in the sun under the window. Once again, the yeast worked in its magical way. The loaves got twice as big as they had been. We put our first two loaves of bread in the oven to bake.

Soon the smell of baking bread spread through the kitchen, the whole cabin, and out through the chinks between the logs. A warm, satisfying, delicious smell.

We had never realized how many workmen went up and down Birchwood Road. From the time the smell of baking bread floated through the air, a man with a road grader pulled into our drive and stopped. He said he wanted to use the phone. Then the electricity man stopped and wanted to make sure we had electricity. A trucker stopped and asked for directions. No one needed directions on only one road.

But each time we answered the door, there was a different man there. While they spoke to us, their eyes were looking past us, toward the kitchen. They said, "You baking bread?" Just as if the smell of baking bread hadn't lured them in the first place.

Somehow, they all had enough time to spare till the bread came out of the oven. The bread was so fresh, it squished under the pressure of the knife. We tore off chunks instead. We got out homemade raspberry jam and butter.

From then on, we baked bread every day just as a matter of routine. Mostly we made white bread. But we made rye bread, too, and whole wheat, cinnamon bread with raisins, banana bread with nuts, and long loaves of French bread that we put straight from the oven into a draft so the crust would crack and butter could be put into the crack to melt. We made sweet rolls with raspberry jam for filling. For New Year's, we made Swedish Tea rings with the dough formed into a roll with butter and cinnamon inside, and then cut in slices that spread out like a fan, all frosted and sprinkled with nuts.

We had a wonderful time.

Someone else who liked homemade bread was Bill. He sat at the dining-room table with his parka on and the dining-room chair tilted back. Whenever Bill was there, we just went on with our work, whatever that was. We poured his first cup of coffee and set the bread and the bread knife in front of him, and the butter and jam. From then on, he took care of himself.

Bill worked mostly part time with his brother, Jesse, who had a back hoe. He worked but never really put his heart in it. He never discussed construction jobs or digging trenches. He was a woods-wanderer. He kept food on his table by hunting small game and fishing. When he talked at all, hunting and fishing and the woods were what he talked about.

Sometimes he would bring us a brace of rabbits, cleaned but with the head and fur left on. Pat, who was almost two and had been raised wrong, liked dead rabbits better than dolls and teddy bears. She would haul one around the house behind her all day long, till it was dinnertime, and then we ate her rabbit. She also loved rabbits for dinner. Rabbits, to Pat, were adaptable. They were playmates and delicious all at the same time. And Bill kept bringing her new ones.

After Bill and Annie, his wife, moved into the trailer across the road from us, we found that Annie was pretty cranky about a lot of things and Bill did like a practical joke now and then.

They didn't have indoor plumbing either and used an outhouse like the rest of us. One day Bill got his hands on a black bear skin. He didn't say anything, but that night before he went to bed, he took the skin out from where he'd had it hidden and took it out to the outhouse. There he tacked it up on the wall so it looked like a bear standing up on its hind legs.

Bill went back to the trailer, and Annie went to the outhouse. She was carrying a lantern. As she opened the outhouse door, there stood a big black bear in the shadows. The light from the lantern hit the skin and made it look as though it was moving. Annie let out a screech, threw the lantern at the bear, and raced squawking all the way back to the trailer.

Maybe it wasn't too funny a joke, but we laughed just the same when Bill told us. Bill never did laugh out loud. He just sort of leaned back and chuckled quietly to himself. You would never have spotted him for a practical joker, if you hadn't known. Bill and Annie didn't stay together very long.

Along toward the end of September, we had a chilly, rainy night. At breakfast the next morning, we looked up from our bowls of oatmeal to the mountain above us. The mountain had changed during the night. In the valley, around our house, the foliage was gray and brown, except for the pine trees scattered here and there. The mountain yesterday had been gray and brown too, with splashes of green from the pines.

The next morning, the top of the mountain was white. We had a moment of panic. Something was wrong. But then we realized that the white we saw was snow. Snow had come to our mountainside when we slept during the night.

Alaskans called the first snow in the higher elevations "Termination Dust." Termination Dust signaled the end of the fall. Winter was coming. We could watch it come down the mountain a little more each time we had rain at night.

Finally, the snow was no longer only on the mountain. The snow was on Birchwood Road too. And on the steep-pitched roof of our cabin. Outside the windows of the cabin, snow flurries blew on a raw wind. By the end of September, we were in an Alaskan winter again.

In October, Wes and Bill went hunting caribou. Bill had got word from somewhere that the caribou were moving. This meant that small bands of caribou, a dozen or so in each group, were moving to form a great herd of thousands that would migrate from beyond the Brooks Range above the Arctic Circle to winter feeding grounds to the south.

The men went north and east of Palmer to Tok Junction. Tok Junction hooked up with the Alcan. They got to Forty Mile Lodge just south of Tok late in the afternoon. It was too dark to hunt, so they slept that night on the floor of the gas station for five dollars apiece. Forty Mile Lodge was crowded during hunting season.

About eight o'clock next morning, when it started to get light, Wes and Bill left the lodge and went looking for caribou. Each man was allowed two.

Caribou are reindeer. The caribou moving now were called Barren Ground caribou. They were smaller than the Woodland caribou that would join into another massive herd and move later in the season. Caribou are handsome animals. Only elk are more beautiful, but elk were in Wyoming and we had the caribou.

Both bulls and cows have racks. But the racks of caribou despite their size, are more delicate and fancy than the wide, flat racks of the bull moose. The bull caribou also has an extra rack. This extra rack is called a spade and goes right down the middle of his forehead, between his eyes. The spade looks a lot like the broad axe used by knights in medieval times. A caribou's hooves are splayed out so they can travel easily over bogs or heavy snow. A caribou is a fine-looking animal.

Just a short distance from Forty Mile, the men saw a

dozen caribou close to the road. While Wes stopped the car, Bill jumped out and dropped four cows with four shots. Cows were better to eat than bulls.

The drive up to Forty Mile and back to Chugiak took two days. Cleaning the caribou took an hour. The hunt had taken about one minute.

By the time the caribou were cleaned and loaded on the roof of the car, other bands of caribou had crossed the road ahead of the car, behind it, and went running alongside. The caribou were moving all right. The migration of the caribou herds was one of the greatest sights in the Territory.

Though the days were shorter now and the snow was on the mountain and the ground around the cabin, temperatures had been pretty mild for Alaska. But on the drive home, a freezing rain began to fall. The road turned to a sheet of ice. The men sat silent in the car. The only sound was the rattling of the plastic that we had put over the rear window of the car to take the place of the pane that had got knocked out.

The men had to drive over Sheep Mountain. On a clear day, Sheep Mountain was beautiful. There was a lodge that looked like lodges are supposed to look. On the driveway up to the lodge were telescopes you could look through to see the Dall Sheep and the mountain goats on the crags. But this day, Sheep Mountain was formidable.

The ice-glittering road ran along the edge of a cliff with a two-thousand-foot drop to the bottom. The cliff looked as if it had been sliced straight down by a great knife at the beginning of creation. The land at the bottom was tundra, flat and treeless with a small stream meandering through the hummocks. In summer, the tundra would have been covered with flowers. Now, on this dismal October day, it was brown and barren.

The road curved and doubled back and curved again.

There were no guard rails. Looking out from the road on the expanse of air and fog before them, the men could see the freezing rain falling two thousand feet below the road to coat the sedges and dead grasses of the tundra with ice.

Steering the car was close to impossible. The car slid slowly toward a hairpin curve. At the outer edge of the curve was a black-and-yellow sign. The sign meant "Do not Go Beyond This point" and is used in the States to show detours or road construction. But as the car slid sideways past this curve, the men saw that beyond the sign was neither construction or detour. Just a straight drop down and a view across miles of tundra to faraway mountains almost hidden in mist and sleet. A few small rocks kicked loose from the edge of the road and disappeared. No one in the car looked to see where the rocks went. The men stared only at the road ahead.

Wes and Bill didn't get home until late that night, but they didn't care. They had gotten across Sheep Mountain. That was the main thing.

The next morning, Bill took his two caribou down to his trailer. We hung ours up on the log ladders at the ends of the cabin. We all set about with the butchering. Wes used a small saw and a butcher knife. We cut the caribou into steaks and chops and roasts. Bill ground the hamburger. We were wrapping pieces of caribou in butcher's paper all through the cabin—in the kitchen, on the dining-room table, and on the coffee table in the living room. We held back a big caribou steak for dinner that night.

The steak was awful. From the time it started to sizzle in the pan, we hated the smell. We hated the taste. Grandma said the meat needed a marinade to take away the gamey flavor. Grandma was apt to come up with the right thing at the right time. We ate peanut butter sandwiches that night, and Grandma put the next night's steaks in a marinade. But nothing could kill that taste.

Some Alaskans loved caribou. Bill did. But we weren't one of them. We gave our caribou to Bill.

The freezing rain that had come down over Sheep Mountain was a warning for us in the valley that bad weather was coming. In a few days, snow piled up deep around the cabin. We stayed snug and dry. Or so we thought until we noticed that the walls at the ends of the cabin were glistening. The glistening look came about because the walls were soaking wet with little drops of moisture running down now and then.

The pitched roof kept most of the upstairs floor dry, except where snow drifted in the open ends. Then the snow melted from the warmth of the downstairs and soaked down onto the walls below. We had thought we were through building until spring, but once we knew the walls were soaking wet, we got chilly just looking at them.

We bought studs and nails, a window for each end, and more log slabs from Mr. Barnhardt. Now we worked with parkas on and heavy boots and thick working gloves. When we climbed the ladder to the upstairs, the edge of the floor was covered with thick ice at the base of the drifts. We had to be careful about slipping.

We cracked the ice on the floor with a pick and shoveled the broken chunks of ice and the snow drifts down onto the ground below. Then we put in studs every sixteen inches across the open ends. We left spaces for the windows. Only this time, we measured the windows and the frames and the space. And this time, as they say in fairy tales about the glass slipper, it fitted her exactly. Or, rather, the windows and the frames fitted exactly into the openings without Wes having to use his saw again.

Before the windows went in, we had climbed up the ladder, slung one leg over the sill, and we got into the upstairs that way. Once the windows were in, we crawled in through a tiny space we had left open under the roof. We didn't dare open up the top of the stairway Slim had built until the outside walls were in place.

For the outside walls, we used Mr. Barnhardt's log slabs. We nailed them in vertically instead of horizontally. Now even wind-driven snow would slide down. Besides, the outside of the cabin looked handsome with vertical slabs on the upstairs.

When the upstairs was sealed in, Wes went up the ladder one last time and crawled through the little corner that we had left open under the eaves. This time he carried a skill saw. He would cut away the floorboards at the top of Slim Land's stairway and open the stairs to the second floor.

Opening up the stairway may not have ranked as high as moving day, but it came close. Neither Grandma nor the kids had ever seen the second floor. They had stood on the ground and waved at us. They had heard us walking around overhead. But they had never been upstairs.

Once Wes had climbed the ladder with the skill-saw and disappeared into the upstairs, we all ran back into the cabin. We crowded in together at the top of the stairway, with our heads just about touching the ceiling. We heard Wes cross the floor, stop above us, and then we heard the whirring noises of the saw.

We were absolutely quiet and waited. Soon the tip of the saw showed through into the downstairs. We all applauded. Wes kept sawing.

Because the tar paper had been pulled off, Wes could look down through the cracks in the floor. He could spot the big beam by the oil stove and the joist nailed to it. He cut the upstairs floor, using the joist as a guide. Then he cut across the floorboards right under the edge of the steep-pitched roof. He cut back to the top of the stairs, following the joist above the walnut wall. By now, he had cut three sides of a long rectangle. The boards he had cut began to sag down onto the stairs. Then, carefully, at the top of the stairs, he gently cut one board at a time. We caught the first board as it fell and carried it out of the way. Then another board. And another, until the upstairs was open.

The kids raced up the stairs to the second floor. Grandma went slower but she was just as tickled. We all rattled around the bare space and looked out the windows, getting a new view of our land. The kids ran round and round the chimney that went right through the second floor and up through the roof.

Then we went outside and nailed the last two slabs in place over our crawl-in corner. We took down the ladder from against the outside wall. We didn't need a crawl-in corner or a ladder any more. We had a two-story log cabin.

We had done a lot that month. We had gotten caribou and tried it and found we didn't like it at all.

Our stairs no longer went nowhere. The upstairs was still a big, empty space with only the chimney in it going up through the roof beyond. We could still look up and see the roof rafters and the ridgepole high above us. We could still see the studs around the windows. We could look between the floorboards in to the rooms below. But from the outside, we looked as though we had an upstairs and a downstairs to live in.

We had done a lot. And we rested.

But we hadn't realized until we happened to look closely at the kids one day, that they had outgrown all the clothes they had and that all our flannel shirts were out at the elbows and frayed from all the work we'd been doing.

We had to do shopping that was long overdue and would still be longer by the time what we bought arrived in the mail.

Twice a year at Marie MacDowell's little Post Office at Moosehorn, we would get, free, in the mail, big thick catalogs from Montgomery Ward's and Sears and Roebuck. We got the Spring/Summer catalogs and the Fall/Winter ones. They came far enough ahead of Spring/Summer and/or Fall/Winter so that we could spend hours every day making choices of what we would order.

Our only alternative was Monty's. Instead of standing in Monty's dreary shop with the salesman who hated us, we sat at home, watching the snow come down while we ate frosted cookies and had coffee and ordered from the catalog.

We could have ordered anything we wanted, provided we could pay for it, from andirons to xylophones and zithers and everything in between. Bathroom fixtures, tools, guns, furniture and, of course, clothes for us all. Our needs were simple. But needs plus wants made catalog shopping complicated but pleasant.

A catalog was called the Wish Book. They always enclosed a lot of order blanks, and it was a good thing they did. We were always luxurious for the first round of selections. We put down everything anybody had ever dreamed of having plus stuff we'd never considered before until Sears/Ward's put it into our heads. We always ended up (Fall/Winter) ordering long johns, flannel shirts, and flannel-lined jeans, and that was about it. But to get to that point, we had to bypass what we had looked at, written on the order blank, and scribbled out. Fine china—service for twelve—beaded and cashmere sweaters and high-heeled opera pumps and shag rugs and shower curtains for the bathroom that was to be.

But even after we scribbled out the non-essentials and started a new order blank with catalog numbers and quantity and price all marked in neatly, choosing was still fun. Catalogs had mainly three colors to choose from. Red, blue, and gold. But did we want red or blue or gold plaid lining in our flannel-lined jeans?

Every year we got mad at whomever we'd ordered from last. When our orders arrived, pink slips were always tucked in with the merchandise that finally came to our door. They had check marks on a long list of reasons why we hadn't gotten what we'd ordered after all. Out of stock. Size n/a (not available). Color n/a.

A shipment took six weeks to get to Chugiak from the States. Reordering took another six weeks. Sometimes we were hard pressed to do without. We would say, "Well! We'll never order from THEM again!" and switch to the other catalog for the next season. But they were both alike. So each year we went from Ward's to Sears to Ward's to Sears and so on. But it was a pleasure just the same.

We did splurge a little on our first fall/winter catalog shopping. We ordered forty yards of bright red flannel, rolls of cotton batting as quilt filler, and a skein of bright red yarn to match the flannel. We would make a big thick, red flannel comforter for every bed in the cabin.

We ordered twenty-eight yards of yellow denim for curtains at all the windows. The dry goods section of the catalog had pages and pages of material, but we stuck with flannel and denim because we knew what they were.

Our pots and pans were tacky, and we had no place to hide them. So we ordered a whole set of Revere Ware—pots and pans of all sizes, with lids and glowing copper bottoms. The new pots and pans would hang on the kitchen walls, copper side facing out, in full view. The lids would be lined up on a narrow shelf above the pots and pans. The kitchen would be splendid.

As children in school, we had been taught that heat rises. We hadn't given it much thought since then. But since we had built a barnlike structure for our second floor, we began to understand about heat rising.

The warmth from the oil stove went directly up the wide staircase and then up to the tip of the steep pitched roof where it did nobody any good.

The Eagle River Lumber people were glad to see us again. We bought thirty large rolls of pink fiberglass insulation, a bucket of spackle, one roll of wide tape, a stapler, twenty-two sheets of wallboard, twelve sheets of heavy-grade plywood and gallon of off-white paint, and two paintbrushes. We carried it all upstairs.

From Mr. Barnhardt's leftover rough-cut lumber, we cut forty studs four feet long and twenty-two rafters six feet long. The studs would give us inside walls. The rafters would lower the ceiling. We cut them outside in the snow and carried them upstairs too. We took up nails and hammers and working gloves.

The upstairs floor that had been bare became a lumberyard.

We filled the spaces between the steep-pitched rafters with thick insulation. We stapled insulation snug around the end wall and the windows. The insulation looked pink and fluffy, but we had to wear our thick working gloves to keep tiny glass splinters out of our fingers.

Wes had wired the upstairs long before. Now, every night, we brought up lamps from the living room and worked long past our bedtime.

From the floor to each rafter on the steep-pitched roof, we toe-nailed in a four-foot stud. Once the wallboard was nailed to the studs, we had a four-foot wall running lengthwise down either side of the cabin, instead of having the steep-pitched roof slant right down to the floor. We could tuck beds and chests along our four-foot wall and still keep from cracking our heads on the low overhang. We would have plenty of walking-around room down the middle of the floor.

Each of the six-foot rafters got nailed from one slanted steep pitch rafter on one side to the opposite rafter on the other side. Once the wallboard was nailed to the new rafters, we couldn't look up and see the ridgepole high above us anymore. Now we had an eight-foot ceiling that would hold the heat in lower instead of letting it rise to the tip of the steep-pitched roof.

We used a trimming knife to fit the wallboard around the windows and to cover the end walls.

We worked late each night. We started early again each morning. We could hear Grandma and the kids get up and hear Grandma fixing breakfast downstairs. We could smell the coffee brewing, the bacon and eggs sizzling in the skillet, and the smell of toast made from homemade bread.

We closed off the stairwell above the walnut wall with studs and wallboard. Now we had a little bedroom off to the right of the landing. We had a big bedroom with the chimney going through it off to the left. The big bedroom still opened onto the stairwell. One could have toppled down the stairwell by walking too far across the floor, but no one ever did.

We built a big closet in the little bedroom. The closet had a shelf and a pole for hanging clothes. It didn't have a door, but it looked nice all the same.

We could still look into the downstairs from between the cracks in the upstairs floor. Heat came up through the cracks too. We began nailing our sheets of plywood over the cracks in the floor. After a while, instead of a lumberyard upstairs, we had clean, new plywood floors with only spackle, tape, the gallon of paint, and the two paintbrushes sitting on them.

All the time we had been stapling insulation and nailing up wallboard, our minds had really been occupied with Halloween.

The school was giving a Halloween party. We were all invited.

Sue wore a bright blue skirt made out of material left over from something. We made her a mantilla out of black net held in place by a tall comb made out of cardboard and covered with foil and sequins. I pooled my costume jewelry with Grandma, and we came up with a pair of dangling earrings and bracelets that clattered and shone. Sue was a Gypsy, we said.

Joe wore a black felt vest with sequins over his flannel shirt. He wore an eye patch that he wouldn't keep over his eye but kept pushed up on his forehead. We made Joe a scimitar cut from cardboard and covered with foil and with sequins on the handle. Joe was a pirate.

The gymnasium at school was decorated with orange and black crepe paper decorations all over the place, cut-out black cats at the windows, and skeletons that kicked up their legs when you pulled a string. There were wrinkled apples shipped up from the States to bob for, and there were spooky games to play. We had baked cupcakes with orange frosting, and we all chipped in for orange and black jelly beans in little paper cups.

A contest was held for best costume, and Sue won. Sue got no prize, but we all clapped. Sue was so overcome that she got sick to her stomach. We all packed into the car and drove back down Birchwood Road to our cabin, where things were quieter and not so exciting.

Once the gypsy and the pirate and the baby and

Grandma (who said she was tuckered out) were tucked in bed, car lights pulled slowly into our drive. We unbarred the door and stood in the cold night air to see who was coming. Two little ghosts tumbled from the car and fell in and out of the snowdrifts that lined the walk up to the door. These little ghosts were as fat as they were tall. They wore their sheets over their parkas, hoods, sweaters, and scarves. We propped them up and gave them cookies. Their hoods and sheets kept slipping down over their eyes, so we had to turn them around to head them back in the direction of the car.

We had not known of any other families in our vicinity. We had not expected Trick or Treat. The ghosts bumbled their way back to their silent and watchful mothers who then drove slowly away. Like the dog-that-was-almost-a-bear, they appeared for a moment and we never saw them again. Alaska seemed a place of appearances and disappearances, like the flaring Northern Lights.

We stood in the open door and looked up toward the mountain, pale white even in the darkness. The school with its lit windows was far away up the road. The cabin was alone and quiet in the night. Low-hanging clouds parted now and then to show the full moon riding in a black sky above them, and the clouds were tinted pale pink and silvery along the edges when the moon shone through. We looked off to the windless forest and wondered what else was dancing, a stately, somber dance, full of reverence, under that cold and moon-splashed sky.

We looked back over our shoulders into our warm and friendly living room.

From ghoulies and ghosties,
    Long leggity beasties
And things that go bump in the night,
    Good Lord, deliver us.

Whatever there was besides us that dwelt within our log cabin was welcome there.

We went inside and closed the door.

After our holiday on Halloween, we were ready to face the upstairs again. I'd always been pretty adept at promising myself imaginary carrots at the end of the stick. I could say to myself, and better yet, believe it, "When this is over, I'll go to the Virgin Islands." I had sense enough to know I wasn't going to the Virgin Islands, or anywhere else, for that matter. But it made time pass faster.

This time, though, the carrot at the end of the stick was real. Spackle the upstairs. Paint the walls. Then we could move up. We would have two more bedrooms.

Wes had hauled the van packer up to the roof, but I put on the spackle. Wes was part cat. He couldn't stand the feeling of messy spackle sticking to his fingers. Mud pies and clay had always been fine with me. Now I squeezed spackle in the cracks between the sheets of wallboard. I smoothed them off and ran tape along the seams. We let it dry. The walls were ready to paint.

With the gallon of paint between us, and two brushes, the paint went on in a hurry. The kids followed along and wiped up drips and pointed out holidays. A holiday is a spot that you've missed when you're painting. We painted the window trim white, the walls white, and the ceiling white.

When the paint was dry, we moved up the furniture. We put Joe's bed in the little room to the right with the closet. We put Grandma's and Sue's beds in the big bedroom that still opened onto the stairwell on the left. We tucked Pat's crib in the big bedroom behind the chimney. We told her that she lived in the chimney corner.

We hung clothes in the closet. We put the kids' crayon drawings on the wall. We made white curtains from old sheets. We put a braided rug by Joe's bed.

Between Grandma's and Sue's beds, we put a rug made by a great-aunt. The rug was of Persian wool in muted colors. A mighty dragon raged down the length. He was too exotic for the cabin but fit in nicely just the same.

Actually, nothing we put upstairs matched anything else. The braided rug and a small chest in Joe's room came from the Trading Post, where we'd gotten the car. One chest we had refinished came from the house in Seattle. Carved vines ran along the drawers. The dragon rug was an antique. The kids' drawings had been made yesterday. The upstairs was like an Irish stew. Everything we threw into the pot turned rich and fragrant.

We had two bedrooms, warm and colorful, where once we'd had a flat roof covered with tar paper and leaking.

Now the upstairs had more room than we could have believed. We rummaged around in the snow for all our leftover lumber. We built a seven-foot closet along the bathroom wall. Under the tallest part of the stairs, we built shelves six feet high to hold our groceries and dishes. The orange crates were pretty but getting wobbly with daily living.

We put a long bench beside the kitchen door and lined up our six pairs of boots under it. Now everyone had a spot to sit on the long bench and a place to put on his boots. We said this was a mud room.

Finally, we hung a door for the empty room that would

be a bathroom. Once we got water, real faucet water, we would be ready.

We built with such vigor that the downstairs seemed filled with flying chips of wood, the sound of sawing and of nails being pounded in with a hammer.

We had to get the building out of the way

November was hunting month. The first moose season was in August. The second in November. We had waited for the second season lest we lose good meat to spoilage. By November, the meat would not thaw. Our frozen meat would keep all winter.

Also, in November, the Woodland caribou were starting to move to form one massive herd, just as the Barren Ground had done before them. Woodland caribou were bigger than Barren Ground, and Bill wanted to add a couple to his meat cache. We would go along for company and to give Bill a hand with the carcass.

They headed up the Richardson Highway—the road-that-went-North. They passed Gulkana. Gulkana had a name, but there was nothing there but an FAA Station and some guy sitting inside getting weather reports. On that day, he was better off inside than outside. At Gulkana the temperature was forty below zero and winds were blowing at forty miles an hour. Gulkana was only about two hundred miles from Fairbanks and for them, forty below was about normal.

The men were headed for Rainy Pass where the caribou had been reported. Ever closer to Fairbanks, the weather was savage.

At Rainy Pass, a small band of caribou moved along the Susitna River on the left of the road. Wes fired a shot at a cow close to the parked car. She paid no attention. He fired again and once again. The cow remained standing, unconcerned. Bill dropped her with a single shot. Wes made plans to sight in his new rifle. This was the only caribou they took. By the time the caribou had been cleaned, the carcass was frozen and the men were, too.

The men rested for a few seconds before loading the carcass onto the roof of the car. They watched the river, flowing swiftly enough so that ice formed only along its banks. They looked at the foothills of the mountains that rose beyond the river.

Suddenly they had the feeling that the ground beneath them was moving slowly upstream. But the ground was not what moved. They saw that thousands upon thousands of caribou covered the foothills. They had been grazing. Now they began moving south. The whole mountain looked as if it were moving as well. The cold and the wind and numbed hands and frosted faces were forgotten as the two men stood there and watched. The caribou did not run. They were not stampeding. They moved south with the deliberation of the ages, past the two men who seemed only small shadows on the edge of the river.

After the men got home and the butchering and wrapping were complete, Wes went down to the rifle range to sight in his gun. We all went along. The range belonged to the Isaac Walton League and was right next to the mud flats. Most of the time, there was no one there but us. It was as quiet and pretty a place as you'd want to see.

Dick Hannon lived down there. He was a caretaker for the Isaac Walton League. They gave him a Quonset hut to live in and a little salary to help out with his pension. Dick was old by any standard, even when we first moved there. He loved the range too.

Dick kept the Quonset hut neat and the grounds neat. He made stone walls and planted ferns along them and stone walks with flowers running alongside. He built a smoke house for smoking salmon caught by members of the League. He built wooden swings to swing on and wooden garden chairs to sit on.

The range itself was one hundred yards long. We stood under birch trees on a lawn that was soft and green in summer but piled high with snow this day. Wes shot down toward the Inlet at a row of posts with cardboard bull's-eyes tacked to them. The only way you knew what you'd hit and what you hadn't was to walk the hundred yards down to the bull's-eye and see for yourself.

The bull's-eyes were interesting. They were the reason that you were there. But just beyond the posts was a little bank that sloped right down to the Knik Arm. You could stoop down and put your hand in the water. The bank was covered with flowers in summer. The Arm went all the way to the horizon. Behind you were flowers.

In November, the bank was covered with snow. So was the rifle range. The Arm was dull gray and flat. There wasn't a ripple on it. But the air smelled of clean snow and the wood smoke from the wood stove in Dick Hannon's Quonset hut.

On this day, Wes found out that his new rifle was shooting three feet high and off to the right. No wonder everything he shot at was safe. He got this fixed, and we all went home.

Except for Joe. Joe stayed down at the range to play cribbage with Dick Hannon.

Dick played a fine game of pinochle. Once a week he came to our house and we played Cut Throat. But better than pinochle, he loved cribbage. Since none of us could play, he taught Joe.

In summer, they played cribbage sitting on the garden chairs, by the ferns and flowers. In fall and winter, when the winds were howling and the snow was blowing, they played cribbage sitting next to the little pot-bellied stove with the fire showing through a little glass door on its front. They ate store-bought cookies, always the same kind, while they played. Fat, round cookies with bright pink icing and a marshmallow layer just under the frosting.

While Joe and Dick Hannon played cribbage that afternoon, Wes and Bill went hunting again. This time they didn't take the car. They were after some local moose. They snowshoed their way up along Peter's Creek above Bill's place.

About a half mile along, a big bull moose stood eating brush. Only bulls could be taken. Killing a cow was illegal. This bull paid no attention to the men. Moose rarely did. They were so big they had few enemies. But this bull moose had two. Wes's rifle had been fixed. He killed the moose with a single shot.

The men dressed the carcass, and each man laced one quarter to his back pack. Each quarter weighed about two-hundred pounds. Bill walked ahead of Wes. They did not talk. Carrying the weight took all the breath they had. Suddenly, the tip of one of Wes's snowshoes caught under a tree root. He went facedown in the deep snow with two hundred pounds of moose strapped to his back.

Bill kept right on walking, heading home. As far as he knew, Wes was right behind him. He got to his trailer and slipped out of the straps on his pack before he realized he was alone. In a panic, Bill headed back to the carcass. By now, Wes had managed to turn over and was now lying on his back with the pack under him. This was actually the way a pack was loaded. The meat was laced to the pack and the hunter lay down on it, face up. He pulled the straps over his shoulders, shifted to a crawling position, and finally stood upright.

So Wes was on the right track. Once Bill knew that Wes was all right, he helped him stand up, dusted the snow off Wes's front, and then leaned against a tree and laughed.

The other two quarters were gotten without any problems. They didn't bother to bring in the big rack. There was nothing edible on it anyway. A serious Alaskan hunter didn't fool with trophies.

We cut and wrapped the moose, just as we had done the caribou. We put the packages of moose into a big wooden crate with a lid on it in the backyard. The crate would be our freezer. Also, the crate would be our protection against marauders.

There were no wolves where we lived. We had heard it said down at Eagle River that if one walked back into the foothills of the Chugach Mountains, sometimes one could see wolves in the distance, playing like dogs in the sunshine. We had no wolves around the cabin, but we were getting neighbors who had sled dogs. We could hear the huskies howling at night, especially when the moon was full. Their howls sounded eerie and strange but grand all the same. We were glad to have them around. But if they decided to come to our house, we wanted our moose safe and secure in its wooden box.

Moose meat was different from caribou. Moose looked like beef and smelled like beef when it was cooking. There was no need to talk of marinade. Moose tasted like beef, only better. Of the whole family, only one of us could not eat moose. While Grandma and Wes and the kids cleaned their plates, I alone ate only vegetables. Sometimes I filled in with pasta. But I never could separate the great and beautiful beast that I saw moving slowly through our woods from the piece of flank, or leg, or whatever it was, that lay browning in the frying pan, no matter how good it looked or smelled.

Last Christmas, we had been in an almost empty house in Nunaka Valley. A house without furniture. A house without Grandma. None of us had heard of Chugiak.

This year we had two and a half acres, except it wasn't paid for yet. Our two-story log cabin was full of furniture. And Grandma walked through the rooms.

Christmas started early for us. No sooner had we cleared the table after Thanksgiving dinner than we all pulled on our parkas and scarves and mittens and boots and went into our own woods to cut us a tree. We would have our Christmas tree before anybody in Alaska or the States had Christmas trees. This tree would have grown on our own land. It was ours.

Walking through the woods was tricky. We couldn't spot roots or stumps or dead vines under the snow that stayed fresh and unwalked on all winter long. We tripped and stumbled. The cuffs of our mittens and our boots got filled with snow.

Most of the trees were big, with their branches *shooshing* in the wind far above us. But down on the quiet floor of the forest, we spotted a tree that looked small indeed by comparison. We cut this tree down and dragged it behind us back to the cabin.

We decorated our country Christmas tree with ornaments we'd bought in the city—Seattle or Miami or Chicago. Then we made strings of popcorn and cranberries. Popcorn and cranberries fell off the strings and got around into the rug. Our tree glittered with too many lights, too much tinsel, and too many strings of popcorn and cranberries. It was exactly right.

The tree filled a corner of the living room. In the early darkness, our tree lights shone out to a snow-covered Birchwood Road.

Come snow, we didn't get out much. Wes brought the

groceries and the mail home with him. The yellow bus took care of Sue. Everything came to our door. We stayed inside. A snowy isolation gave us a Christmas world.

In that sequestered world, we told Pat about Santa Claus. We started him off as a bedtime story. We backed him up with pictures from a book. We learned to recite. We could repeat all of the stanzas from "Night before Christmas," including the part about "as dry leaves that before the wild hurricane fly, when they meet with an obstacle, mount to the sky. . . . " Santa Claus walked through our rooms as surely as we did. He had a broad face and a round little belly. He wore a red suit. For one season, a mythical being lived at our house. Best of all, there was nobody to say he wasn't real.

One evening, Wes brought home the groceries. In one of the brown sacks was a little magazine put out by the Piggly Wiggly people. On the cover of the magazine were the prettiest Christmas cookies we'd ever seen—stars and trees and snowmen and some red-and-white ones shaped like candy canes.

Inside the magazine was the recipe.

Next morning, we got out our breadboard. We found cookie cutters that we'd forgotten we had, and a heavy rolling pin as well. The recipe said it made six dozen. We didn't believe them. We quadrupled the recipe.

We filled the biggest bowl that we had with batter. Soon we had cookies cut out in shapes, waiting to go in the oven. We had two tins of cookies baking at the same time. We had cookies cooling in long lines on the dining-room table. We colored some batter red and twisted it in stripes around the plain batter to make the candy canes.

Long after the kids were asleep that night, Grandma and I still sat at the dining-room table. We iced dozens upon dozens of cookies. Our backs ached with the sitting, and our eyes watered from fatigue.

But when the kids got up the next morning, the cabin was full of frosted and decorated cookies. We looked like a bakery shop. We had pink trees and green trees, pale blue stars, white snowmen, bells that were golden, and red candlesticks tipped with gold for a flame. We piled them in bowls and put them on trays. The candy cane ones we hung on the tree.

One of the best things about that Christmas was that we didn't have to budge from the cabin even to buy presents. The cabin was present enough for the adults. Along with the flannel-lined jeans we had ordered for the kids from Ward's last fall, we had ordered books and games and kept them hidden under the bed for Christmastime.

Pat was too small to know the price of things. We made her a doll out of a white sock with brown yarn for hair. The doll was soft and plump, with button eyes and an agreeable grin embroidered on. We made the little creature a dress and a nightie with ribbons. Because we were being lavish that season, we made the doll a cradle out of an oatmeal box cut in half. We made a soft mattress, a pillow trimmed in lace, and a red flannel comforter like the rest of us had.

Christmas morning came and went with a rush and left us with a floor covered with wrapping paper. We had a homemade Swedish tea ring on the dining-room table for later. Right now we dunked in fresh coffee our candy-cane cookies that had turned to rock hanging on the tree, while we got our wits about us.

Pat talked and talked to her doll. Pat also talked to dead rabbits and invisible playmates. We were glad the doll measured up to her standards, whatever they were. The kids played with their new games.

Christmas morning was like a Fourth of July Rocket or a

Roman Candle. It lit the cabin with stars and colors and disappeared.

By the time winter came, we had made thick red flannel comforters for all the beds. We had gold denim short curtains at all the windows. We had a row of shining copper-bottomed pots and pans hanging on a wall in the kitchen. The house smelled of baking bread and Christmas cookies. We looked and smelled warm and cozy. But these were only sights and smells.

We froze the first winter. The upstairs was warm. All the heat still went upstairs, and now it stayed there. But downstairs, we froze. Floorboards and a rug weren't enough to keep out the cold air. Next year we would bank the house, piling dirt around the base of the cabin and covering the first two logs, but we didn't know about that this year until the ground was frozen solid and under deep snow. The snow didn't really bank the house because enough heat escaped from the cracks between the floorboards and the chinks between the logs to melt the snow around the edges. So we had icy winds moving under the cabin all winter long.

Next year, we would install a heatilator, a little device that fitted into the stove pipe, like a fan. It would suck in cold air and blow it out. We hadn't known about a heatilator before either. We could stay warm downstairs only if we stood close to the oil stove or opened the oven door to take something out that had been baking.

We wore flannel shirts with sweaters on top, long johns and flannel-lined jeans and woolen socks and furry slippers. We still froze. Someone was always standing hunched next to the oil stove, stretching their hands over the steaming big kettle and trying to get warm for a little while. We dressed and undressed by the stove and had burns on our bottoms to prove it. This happened to all boondock Alaskans, it seemed. Even cartoons in the newspapers showed grizzled Alaskans in long johns being pretty sprightly after backing into a hot coal stove, and oil stoves were no better either. Alaskans thought it was pretty funny once they got through hopping around the room. It went with the territory, Alaskans said.

Along around the middle of winter, hunters, who were running low on meat in the cache, began watching the sky and listening to weather reports for news of an oncoming snowstorm. Moose-hunting season was in August and again in November. But poaching filled the cache in winter, and poaching was best done at the onset of a big snow.

A lone hunter had to be crafty because the government of Alaska was a wily hunter too. The government used spotter planes—little single-engine planes flying low with a pilot looking out the window for traces of an illegal kill. In the cabin we got used to the occasional drone of a light aircraft, making slow circles overhead, checking out remote cabins and the forests below. So a silent battle took place through the snow-laden wilderness and into the slate-gray skies.

A hunter willing to risk both license and fine for moose meat that was now lean and tough rather than fall prime was a pretty serious man. He wasn't joking around. When the clouds began to hang low, he took notice.

Spotter planes flew until a storm closed in. The hunter sat in his cabin with his ear next to the radio, learning how soon the snow would come, how much snowfall to expect, and when the storm would be over. The last thing he wanted was to get halfway through the kill only to have the skies brighten and leave him standing next to a carcass with blood staining the snow. He needed a bad enough storm to give him time to finish his business and cover his tracks and the carcass, too.

The hunter's gun was clean anyway, but he checked it over, put his snowshoes by the door and his wool socks close to the heater to get warm. He and his wife didn't discuss hunting. When he finally opened the door and stepped into the falling snow, any questions about "Where is Daddy going?" got a short "Out!" for an answer. Nobody wanted a second-or third-grader going to school bragging that his father had got a moose last night.

For days before the storm, the hunter had his eyes out for moose sign. He knew where the usual trails were. He followed tracks and checked for fresh spore. He knew what he was after. Once the storm hit, the hunter worked against time, with his rifle and his backpack and his hunting knife, working in a blizzard and into the night.

That was how poachers behaved. We never did find out what game wardens did during a storm. Probably took it easy. There wasn't much else they could do. But as soon as the storm eased off, the spotter planes made their slow, efficient circles again.

Some hunters had fresh meat in the cache. Some did not.

There never was any excitement to the hunt as far as we were concerned. Or as far as anybody else we knew was concerned either. Alaskan hunters did not band together as hunters in the States are inclined to do—talking about the thrill of the hunt over a case of beer. Alaskan hunters were no-nonsense. They wanted meat. That was all there was to it. They pulled on their oldest, raggediest jeans and parkas. They took a sandwich in a pocket and hoped they wouldn't be gone long enough to need it.

Slaughtering a moose was nothing much to get enthused about. The hunt had no more thrill in it to a serious hunter than buying staples at the Piggly Wiggly. Just a lot more hard work.

After years of eating moose almost exclusively, barring a few pork chops now and then and a turkey for Thanksgiving, our hunting habits and our eating habits suddenly changed.

On a sunny afternoon in the hunting season, a sleek young bull walked onto our land. He had followed the same trail past our cabin as the cow and calf during the spring when we were raising the cabin walls. But instead of disappearing into the woods beyond, he stayed with us, eating still tender forage right at the edge of our clearing. The sun was warm on his back, and he was fat and content. He just stood there and ate.

Finally, after watching him from the window and expecting him to move away, Wes loaded his rifle and eased his way around the side of the cabin toward the bull until he was only about seventy feet away. The bull was aware of the movement and of Wes, but he was feeling peaceful and lazy in the mild afternoon. He watched Wes and then started eating again. For us, getting a moose this close to the cabin would have eliminated a lot of backpacking. It was too good a chance to be missed.

When Wes raised his rifle, we turned away from the window and covered our ears, but we heard the single rifle shot anyway. Minutes later, Wes came back into the house to get his hunting knife. His face was lined and gray. His hands shook. There was no talk of meat for the table. There was no talk at all. We worked to quarter the carcass in a dreadful silence. Finally Wes said, "He just stood there." That was enough.

After we finished our work, Wes told us what had happened. As he raised his rifle, the moose had turned and looked at him. The shot got the moose between the eyes, clean and deadly. Blood jutted in an arc from the wound. The bull did not fall. He looked at Wes. He looked kind and gentle, and he never took his eyes off Wes. Finally his great legs buckled and he went down. He was dead.

In those seconds that seemed like forever, Wes said all he could think about was a ptarmigan he had shot on a nameless island of Gustavus early in fall. Wes had gone down on board an FAA plane that was checking the ILS (Instrument Landing System). He had taken his rifle, hoping to get a deer once the day's work was over.

No deer were to be seen. But he and another crewman spotted a ptarmigan eating seeds and berries about seventy-five yards away. The crewman, who hadn't brought a gun, said, "Boy! I'd really like that ptarmigan in a pot for dinner tonight."

Wes raised his rifle and killed the bird. The shot was beautiful. One moment the bird was eating berries. The next moment his neck was broken and he was on his way to a stew pot.

Wes had been raised on a farm. He knew that the beef we ate came from some steer, loaded onto a truck and shipped to a slaughterhouse hundreds of miles away. But he hadn't pulled the trigger for that steer. He hadn't watched him, sitting, like the ptarmigan, eating berries. In the midst of all the congratulations for a fine shot, Wes said all he could think of was *Where did I get the right?*

"Where did I get the right?" was Wes's own personal question. But he said the moose as it looked at him had asked only "Why?"

After the young bull moose at the edge of our clearing, we never hunted again.

During the winter, we had more time to read. Now and then, Wes brought home, from somewhere, a stack of old copies of the *Christian Science Monitor*. I didn't care how old they were. They were better than boxes of chocolates.

The *Monitor* had a reputation for excellence in reporting both domestic and international news. I skipped all that. I headed straight for the sections on Art and Literature.

I got out my scissors and cut out a picture of a stripey cat playing a flute painted by a artist in ancient Japan. I read about Ben Franklin saying, "Mark how luxuries encroach," when his wife finally gave him his porridge in a china bowl instead of his usual wooden one. I read a fine article about spatter floors in old colonial houses. I coveted their spatter floors.

On this snowy night, there was a knock at our front door. Bill was standing on our doorstep. He was supporting a wooden box. The box was made of dark brown planks and was taller than Bill was. It was about eight feet long two feet wide, and three feet high. Bill said, "I got you a pipe box." Then he looked sheepish and said, "I can take it away if you don't want it."

I never could pass up a wooden box. One never knew when they might come in handy. We had used orange crates for kitchen cabinets. I used little wooden Kraft cheese boxes, stacked up, to keep our spices in. Bill's box had hauled pipe all the way from the States. The pipe was gone, but the box leaned, brown and handsome and heavy, against the cabin. As a box, it commanded respect and admiration.

Now, with all of us pushing and pulling, we dragged the box into the cabin until it rested halfway through the living room and halfway into the dining room. We had to move chairs to make enough room. The box was magnificent, all right, but suddenly we wondered what it was doing in the middle of the cabin. We looked at Bill.

Bill was high-class scrounger. He could spot quality a

mile off. He never scrounged unless a thing was exactly right. Bill said, "It's for your kitchen sink."

We didn't have a kitchen sink. We had a tin dish pan. Then, suddenly, we saw what Bill had already seen. A counter between the kitchen and the dining room and with a sink at one end. We were so overwhelmed that we just gaped. Now we pulled and shoved with purpose until the box was in place and we had an L-shaped kitchen with a wide counter separating the kitchen from the dining room.

Bill still wasn't through. He went back outside and brought in two pieces of a heavy composition material, not wood but probably longer lasting. He had hauled them to our door too. He said, "You need a kitchen floor." Each section was five feet wide by ten feet long. He laid them side by side over our rough wood floor with cracks in it. Suddenly we had an L-shaped kitchen ten feet square as though it had been transported from the pages of *House Beautiful.*

The awe and excitement of the evening had proved tiring. We slumped in chairs around the dining-room table. We drank coffee. Nobody talked. Then, out of the quiet, an idea floated over our coffee cups, like a tangible thing.

We would spatter the floor.

The next day we bought a sink against the day when we would have water in the kitchen. Wes borrowed the skill-saw again. This time, he cut a hole in the top of the pipe box to fit the sink about one-third of the way down the box. Now we had counter space alongside the stove. Then came the sink. Then a long counter, two feet wide, to put dinner plates on and pass them over to the dining room. Or to mix bread dough on. Or to put a bowl of flowers from the mud flats on, when summer came again. We favored luxury encroaching, no matter what Ben Franklin said.

For nights, after everyone was in bed, we worked to spatter the floor. First the floor got painted with three coats of beige. Each one had to dry. Then we bought everybody new toothbrushes because we needed the old ones to do the spattering. We bought half-pints of green and red and blue and bright yellow paint. Then, dipping somebody's old toothbrush into the half pint of blue, we shook the brush and little drops of blue splattered onto the beige floor.

With each shake, we were purely afraid lest we shake off just a common looking blob and ruin the whole effect. But it never happened. Each fleck and drop of blue paint landed perfectly. We let the floor dry overnight.

The night after that, we spattered red. Then green. Then bright yellow. After a while, we had an L-shaped kitchen with a rich brown counter sitting on a pale beige spatter floor with little drops of blue and red and yellow and green shining all over it.

We had remodeled our kitchen just by answering a knock on our door that snowy night.

Back at his trailer, Bill had a problem. Eddie was his problem. Eddie was a rotten kid. There was no point making excuses for him. He lived down toward Eagle River. He was supposed to be in high school, but he skipped a lot and nobody at the school was keen on finding him or getting him back. So Eddie roamed, up to no good.

One of the places he roamed was Bill's trailer. Bill was like a bear during the winter. He hibernated. He slept a lot while the snow was falling. Eddie thought no one was at home.

The reason Eddie went to Bill's place was that Bill had a fine husky named King on a chain in the backyard. King was a sweet animal, well-fed and well thought of by all who knew him. Except for Eddie. To Eddie, any dog on a chain was fair game and great sport.

Roused from his sleep, Bill heard King raging around

outside. When Bill went to check on him, he found King at the limit of his chain, trying to get at Eddie, who was poking him with a long branch and staying just out of reach. King was about beside himself.

Bill had never met Eddie before. So he explained to him, gently, that this was no way to treat a good dog like King. Eddie seemed contrite and left. Bill figured that was the end of it, but he made inquiries just the same. He found that teasing animals was a way of life for Eddie.

Sure enough, Eddie came back, tormenting King. Again, Bill went out and spoke quietly, telling Eddie again what a good dog King was, in case he didn't know. Another thing Eddie didn't know was that although Bill never raised his voice, inside his head Bill reckoned that this was warning number two. There would be no third warning.

After Eddie left this time, Bill took off King's collar and cut it almost clean through. King was easygoing and well-cared for. He never bothered to pull at his chain. Unless Eddie was around. The collar held together well enough when Bill put it back around King's neck. But one good pull and the collar would break.

Now Bill stayed awake inside the trailer. But he moved his pickup out of the drive so King appeared to be alone. One reason Bill was such a good hunter, and practical joker, too, was that he had the patience of Job. Now he sat inside his trailer behind a curtained window and watched for Eddie. His eyes twinkled and he had a half smile on his face. He just waited.

He waited for a couple of days. Then Eddie came sneaking out of the woods. King bared his teeth and snarled. Eddie was grinning. Inside the window, Bill was grinning now too.

Eddie poked at King with a long stick and then jumped back out of reach of the chain. King, infuriated, lunged against the chain. His collar snapped. Eddie's leer changed to panic. He dropped his stick and headed, screaming, for the nearest tree, which happened to be a scrub pine. Up the tree Eddie went, with King roaring right behind him.

Scrub pines aren't meant to be climbed. The branches of a scrub pine are far apart and not strong enough to bear much weight. Also, scrub pines are not usually terribly tall. So Eddie found himself at the tip of a short pine tree, clinging to thin and stickery branches, a pine that bent toward the ground where King was racing in circles, making savage noises and leaping up at him. And above King's racket, Eddie kept screaming in pure terror.

Bill was never one to hurry. He moved more slowly than usual now. Once he got outside, though, he collected King and helped Eddie, all scratched up, down out of the tree. Eddie was bawling like a baby. Bill lent him a handkerchief. Between the two of them, they examined the broken collar. Bill said, "They don't make collars like they used to. A collar can break just any old time."

After a while, Eddie quit snuffling. He left and walked back up the road. He never bothered King again. As a matter of fact, we heard that he gave up teasing any dog on a chain from then on. As Bill said, "You just never can tell with collars nowadays."

Spring/Summer

Close to a year ago, we had picked out our homesite when the land still lay under deep and heavy snow, just starting to melt around the trees. Now the time had come for us to go back to the Land Office and get clear title to our homesite. We needed proof of building, which was easy because the cabin existed. The cabin was real. But we also needed a two hundred and fifty dollar lump sum to pay for the land. We needed more money than that. We needed money for the well we planned to put in, and the septic tank, and a tub and a sink and a john.

For the past year, we had spent every extra penny, and some that weren't extra at all, on boards and paint and nails and roofing. Even pooling all our resources, we couldn't raise that kind of money. We would have to borrow the money from the bank and use the cabin as collateral.

We celebrated the night before the bank man was to come out. We congratulated ourselves the next morning at breakfast. The bank man would solve all our money problems. We waited for the bank man.

We always kept the cabin and the kids clean. That day they sparkled. Grandma, as usual, was at her best. Grandma had been raised with more formality than the rest of us. Always, at the end of the noon meal and its dishes, she took off her apron, put on a little lipstick, combed her hair, and buttoned on a clean cardigan. Now she was what she called "at home" or ready for company. A butler, if she had one, would have told anyone coming to call that she was "at home," meaning that the visit was acceptable to her. Grandma was ready to "receive" guests. We never had any. But that day Grandma was ready for the bank man. The bank man was to be our honored guest.

He arrived exactly when he said he would. Not a moment sooner or a moment later. He was a tall, middle-aged man with a slight paunch from eating too well. He wore a three-piece suit, gray and tailor-made, and expensive shoes that shone to perfection. He had a jovial manner. He smiled constantly and had the habit of rocking up on his toes and back on his heels as he spoke.

We were going to take him on a prideful tour of our beloved cabin, but he refused. He walked by himself up the wide staircase, glanced to either side of the landing, came back downstairs again, and stood in our living room, smiling and rocking back and forth from heel to toe. Then he said, "You've got nothing here."

Our minds were fixed on assured success and on some praise as well. The steep-pitched roof, the frames around the windows, the kitchen sink and the spatter floor and the view from the dining room window up to the mountain. What we heard was swallowed up in what he had anticipated. I smiled and turned to Grandma and said, "Mom! Did you hear? He said we have . . ." and then it was as though I heard the sound of all the nails, we had hammered in being pounded in at once. The noise racketed through my head. My mind flip-flopped. I couldn't repeat what had been said. But the bank man didn't mind repeating himself at all. "You've got nothing here," he said, and then he left.

Whoever said that Anchorage was the "longest bar in the world" was right. But there was more to Anchorage than that. Anchorage had three banks. Not just one.

The second bank sent out two young men who sat in our driveway in their car and talked between themselves, never looking at the house. They laughed and chatted in an amiable way. We went out to the car to invite them in, but they said there was no need. Then they drove away.

The third bank sent out a young man who had evidently been told what to say before he left the office. He was so embarrassed and apologetic that we felt quite sorry for him.

I felt sorry for Wes, too. Wes sat in an easy chair in the living room with his head in his hands. He said, "Oh, my God! I'm going to end up walking down Birchwood Road with a cabin on my back!"

I felt sorry for Grandma, too. She had dealt with a black bear in the back-yard. She had gone back to living without a faucet to turn on. Now she washed coffee cups that hadn't been used and put them away again. She was wearing her best cardigan for the third time in a row.

I just felt sorry.

Grandma had taught us, along with first impressions and the fact that it takes money to buy whiskey, never to wash your dirty linen in public. No matter how bad we felt, we kept our troubles to ourselves.

But one morning, as I sat at the counter at Moosehorn and stared down into a mug of black coffee, Marie MacDowell came and sat next to me. Marie was an idea-woman. She had a saying of her own. "Great minds discuss ideas, average minds discuss events, small minds discuss people." People never came up when you talked with Marie.

Until this morning. I told Marie our problem. I felt disgraced as I did so. I had been hypnotized by staring into my mug on the counter for so long. Marie's face was usually kind anyway. Now it was kinder than usual. She didn't comment on the evil bank men. She didn't tell me what a great cabin we had. she just listened. Then she put her hands over mine. She said, "Go to Palmer."

Palmer was a little frontier town. Palmer took care of permanent settlers and farmers. Unlike Anchorage, it was not a serviceman's town. Surrounded by mountains and the Arm, Palmer sat on flat ground, without trees. Cabbages grew in the Matanuska Valley, and the red raspberries, we got by the roadside. Palmer had a little hospital and a main street, with a couple of small grocery stores, a hardware shop and a drugstore that also sold gifts and cards for the people who were in the hospital. Palmer had a bank.

Listless from repeating our requirements, we went into the bank. We spoke to the manager. We talked to him across a counter. We didn't even sit down at his big desk. He said, "You got a homesite." We nodded. He asked, "You got a structure on it?" We nodded. Then he asked, "How much do you want?" We signed papers. It wasn't until we were back out on Palmer's little main street that we realized what had happened.

We had money in the bank.

We went to the little drugstore and had ice cream and coffee. From their gift shop, we bought presents for the kids and for Grandma.

The next day, we went to the Land Office in Anchorage for the last time. We paid for the homesite and signed our papers for the government.

The rest of the money we saved for pipes and plumbing and a septic tank. We had gotten cautious, which is what having a little money can do to you. Besides, the Palmer bank man had been friendly once. He might not be friendly twice. We didn't want to take the chance.

We did get out our Sears Catalog, though. We picked

and chose. Finally we decided. We ordered our bathroom fixtures.

Six weeks later, they arrived, crated in wooded boxes. For once, the wooden boxes meant nothing to us. With six people and crated fixtures all crowded together in our would-be bathroom, we got crow bars and ripped the crates open.

Inside, shiny white and pure, was our bathroom furniture. The fixtures gleamed in the sun that came through the bathroom windows. They were worth the six-week wait. They were worth the Palmer bank's money. This was as close to a bathroom as we had gotten in over a year.

The faucets turned on and off. But we had no water. We were, so to speak, "All dressed up with no place to go."

We still didn't have a well. But the ground was starting to thaw. We would begin working on our well the next day.

We wanted our well close to the house, so we just went out the back door and started digging. We could have touched the cabin wall from where we stood. Wes dug and dug and dug. He started out at ground level and dug until we couldn't see the top of his head anymore. He had to dig around great boulders that had lain under the surface of our land since the beginning of time. He split what rocks he could with the sledgehammer, and we hauled them out, piece by piece.

Wes dug until he couldn't throw shovels full of dirt out of the hole because the top of the hole was too far over his head. We rigged a tripod with a bucket on a pulley that could be lowered, filled with dirt and returned to the surfaced to be emptied. But even in mid-spring, glasslike ice rimmed the edge of the crater Wes was digging. When I reached forward to grab the bucket Wes had raised to the top of the tripod, I slipped on the ice and the bucket tipped. A whole bucketful of gravel and cold mud fell back down into the well. Fierce words came roaring from deep in the hole. I couldn't see Wes and was glad I couldn't. I tried again. And again. I never had any success. The weight of the bucket plus the slippery ice made digging and removing the dirt impossible. And we still had no sign of water.

We figured that just because we wanted the well close to the house didn't mean there was water there. We could look out over our land and into the woods and still not have any idea where water was close to the surface.

Then we met a water witcher. Dowser is the right name, but where we lived he was called a witcher. He was a small, gentle man. He wore a stocking cap pulled down over his ears and a long muffler hanging down his back. He came to our door one day and talked, hesitantly, about nothing at all. He was pleasant and kind, and we waited for him to say whatever it was he really wanted to say. Finally, he looked over his shoulder and then all around the room and said, "I can find your water for you." He almost whispered. Then he looked sorry he had said anything at all.

Since the well hadn't come up in the conversation and water-dowsing was the furthest thing from our minds, we had to take a second to right ourselves. We knew that experts claimed water-witching was a superstition. Experts said witching was unscientific and not supported by fact. But we had learned one thing. Find out what the experts say. Then do the opposite. It works better that way. We could have hugged our witcher.

We trailed along behind him with his stocking cap and muffler out to the woods behind the cabin. He took a penknife from a deep pocket in his coat. He cut a thin branch a couple of feet long from a birch tree. The branch had a fork in it. He held either side of the fork like a big wishbone out in front of him. Then he started walking slowly back and forth on our land behind the cabin.

91

We followed paces behind. We kept quiet. There was no wind. There were no bird calls. Just the sound of our boots on the dead brush and the fallen pine needles. But the little witcher, intent on the forked branch in his hands, seemed to be listening for something that we could not hear and waiting for something that we could not see. We walked in the presence of the Unusual.

The tip of the birch branch began to tremble and to bend toward the ground. The witcher stopped on the spot. He held the ends of the branch so tightly that his knuckles turned white. Still the fork quivered and bent till it twisted out of his hands. "Dig here," the witcher said.

We marked the spot with a little heap of stones. Then he repeated the performance just for fun. We all took turns, but the branch stayed still. We watched him again and again, clustering around him, jostling each other, all talking at once. As closely as we watched, there was no doubt about it. The branch moved on its own, like a live thing.

The witcher was enjoying himself. But then he got serious again. He asked Wes for a handsaw. When Wes brought it to him, he held the saw by the handle and extended the blade over our little pile of stones. Soon the tip of the saw began to vibrate. It dipped toward the ground. "Count!" said our witcher. And we did. The blade of the saw dipped down toward the marked spot twenty times. "Dig down twenty feet," said the witcher. "You'll have all the water you need."

Grandma used to say "Unexpected things always turn out best." She was right as usual. An hour ago, we hadn't even met this man. Now for the second time, we stood slack jawed and round eyed. We had used that saw often enough to know it hadn't vibrated and dipped for us.

From his old pickup, the witcher got a piece of iron tied to the end of a rope. He held the rope at arm's length, with the chunk of iron dangling directly over our marked spot.

Slowly the iron began to swing. It moved in a big circle over our little heap of stones. The iron circled twenty times. Then the movement stopped and the iron hung quiet and heavy again. The iron and the saw agreed. Twenty feet down there was water.

Back in the house, sitting around the dining room table, drinking coffee and eating cookies, we picked up amenities that had been left out before. The witcher said his name was Swanson. He was Paul Swanson's father. Paul was the shopkeeper who had sold us our six tomato seeds for fifty cents the spring before. Our witcher was not the elf he appeared to be. He had a name and human ties.

The fifty cents reminded us of money. What did witchers charge? We hadn't asked before because we were afraid to find out. We had decided to leap first and look later, figuring something out when the time came. Now we asked Mr. Swanson for his bill.

"No, no," said our little witcher. "You don't understand." He explained. There was more to witching than just the witching itself. His father had been a witcher, but no one else in his family. He himself could never wear a watch, for instance. They either stopped or told the wrong time. His father had taken him witching with him, sensing his talent. But witching was an art that could not be taught. It was a skill that could not be learned. "Witching," said the little man in all earnestness, "is a gift given directly from God to the witcher." Therefore, it seemed, payment would be a sacrilege. We suggested calling money a gift in return, rather than payment. But he said God would see right through that. To accept money would be to taint the gift and lose it. Freely he had received, he said, and so he freely gave.

He ate our cookies. He drank our coffee. He had given us water. He had let us follow behind him to see a Miracle.

He had come without our asking, and when he left, we never met him again.

This well was easy to dig because we didn't wonder, with each shovelful, if we really should be digging somewhere else. We were sure. This time, there were no boulders to split with the sledgehammer. Even the ground seemed softer.

At ten feet, water began seeping into the well. At twelve feet, we had to rent a suction pump. The water poured in faster than the pump could get it out. We took the pump back. We figured a twelve-foot well was good enough. At twelve feet, we had a wonderful well, a well with pure water, running, clear water. A well that would never run dry.

The saw and the chunk of iron at the end of the rope had erred in their calculations. But they had erred on the side of kindness. Digging eight feet less than one expected to dig is better than digging eight feet more.

In June, Jesse, who was Bill's brother, brought his backhoe down the road, into our drive and around to the back of the house. Jesse would dig our cesspool and the pipe lines from the well to the bathroom and our kitchen.

Jesse was about as different from our little witcher as a man could be. Jesse was big and jovial. He had a broad face and was usually smiling or, at least, ready to smile. Jesse had sired a son also, but his son was just a little boy running around in second grade. He wasn't a seed seller.

Jesse was a hard worker, shifting gears, going forward and backward on his noisy machine, smiling and waving to us, all at the same time. His machine took after him, like a mechanical son. The machine made talking around it impossible, it racketed so. It growled and dug and rode up and down the hills of dirt, it had itself created. Everything was hurry and scurry and great good will.

By the time the septic tank and the pipe lines were dug,

the backyard looked as though some giant mole had gone berserk. The ground was crisscrossed with deep trenches and high mounds of dirt. We had to put a plank across each of the trenches that gaped between the cabin and the little outhouse that was still our bathroom. Hopping along those unsteady planks gave outdoor plumbing an adventurous side that it had never had before.

Once the pipes were laid and Jesse and his backhoe had covered them over, the noise stopped. Inside our quiet house, a new water pump and a new hot water heater waited under the broad stairway to the second floor. These would give us water at a steady rate and hot water to bathe in.

The bathroom waited quietly too. The bathroom had furniture in it—a sink, a toilet, towel racks, a toilet paper holder, a place to hang all our toothbrushes and a tub that had never had a ring in it.

It was time to turn on the water.

We all ran to the bathroom and crowded around the sink. We turned on the faucet. Water came out. Water, pure, clear, full of bubbles and splashes on the wall. Water that circled clockwise in the bottom of the basin and then disappeared forever down the drain. We turned the faucet off. We had just wasted more water than we would have used in days. We turned the faucet on again. The water was still there. Water gushing from a bathroom faucet. Water surging from some underground stream.

Suddenly we felt we owned, not only a surface of two and a half acres of land with trees and bushes sitting on top, but cubic acres of land below the surface. Underground acres past "caverns measureless to man, down to a sunless sea" and perhaps to a fiery core beyond.

We hung the number-two tub on a nail outside the back door. We hung our tin dishpan and the dipper on hooks on the kitchen wall. We emptied our two five-gallon canteens in a rush of water over the cranberry bushes in the backyard. Now and then, when we got thirsty, we still went to the kitchen corner where the canteens had stood on the floor. We looked for the dipper.

But that was all past. It didn't take us long to get used to new ways—or old ways remembered. For a little while, we had gone back in time. That was all. Now we were back in the same age and time as everybody else.

We were a nice family.

Forever in that cabin, a small girl writes "$1.00" on a slip of paper, wads it up, and puts it in the toe of her shoe that sits under her bed. She has gotten a dollar from somewhere and waits for the day when she can write two instead of one. Grandma watches "The Lone Ranger" on TV, sitting where she can see the clock also, lest the Lone Ranger get too exciting and she need reassurance of only so many more minutes left before she knows all will be well. A small boy hides under the stairs that go nowhere and waits for the sound of the cavalry on "Wagon Train," and then he knows it is safe to come out. The littlest child sits on the floor and gently rocks the dead rabbit she holds in her arms.

We were not a Camelot. We had no turrets and pennants or moats to protect us. We had a steeply pitched roof and a chimney. We were surrounded by mountains that rose around us and an ocean that stretched away forever past the horizon.

But surely, even at Camelot, somebody opened the back door and threw the wash water out.

PROPERTY OF
KENAI COMMUNITY LIBRARY